Fight the Good Fight
of Faith

Disclaimer:

The author or publisher assumes no responsibility for errors or omissions. Neither is liability assumed for damages resulting from the use of information contained herein.

F I R S T   E D I T I O N
Published in 2021
www.Unveiled-Ministries.com

Written by: Stephenie Haney Montes |
UnveiledLadiesMinistries@gmail.com

ISBN: 978-0-578-93538-6

Library of Congress Case
Haney Montes, Stephenie
The Fearless Woman
Case Number: 1-10588497131 | June, 2021

Library of Congress Cataloging-in-Publication Data

Category: Christian Living, Motivational & Inspirational, Women in Christ

Cover Design & Formatting by: Eli Blyden | EliTheBookGuy.com

Edited by: Bethany Sledge

Published & Printed in the United States of America | Tampa, Florida

Thanks

To my late father, Kenneth F. Haney, whom I miss immensely. I'm thankful for what he instilled into me at a young age. He had a lot of fire, passion, vision, and tenacity, and some of that has been transferred into me. I find myself often saying, "What would Dad do?" He was always disciplined, prayerful, and focused on reaching the world for Jesus, so that is what I plan on doing too. One day we will meet again. Until then, just know, Daddy, that I am staying the course and fighting the good fight of faith like you taught me to.

To my mother, Joy Haney. When I think of you I see a woman who is fierce as a lion, strong like the wind, and confident like an eagle. Mom, You've been a consistent, positive, and godly voice in my life. I never grow tired of our talks or the words of faith, hope, and life you speak into the atmosphere. You truly are a woman of great faith, and I am thankful that you have instilled such incredible golden nuggets into me. Thank you for being a praying mother who never gave up on me.

To my husband, Asbel. Thank you for being amazing, supportive, and encouraging. You are the sparkle in my life, and I savor each shining moment we have together. Hand in hand, you and I. I . . . love . . . you.

To my sisters, Sherrie, Elizabeth, and Angela. We've been through the good, the bad, and the ugly. But we will continue to stand strong in our faith and to be bold, brave, and fearless women for God. Love you always.

To my brother, Nathaniel. I've watched you trudge forward when your body has been under attack. You never give up but you just keep on going. When the enemy has tried to cripple your faith, you refused to take a back seat, and you continue to walk into your calling. Love you always.

To my editor, Bethany Sledge. Thank you so much for taking time to edit this book. You do everything with excellence.

Thank you to Eli Blyden for your expertise in creating an incredible cover. You truly rock!

Special thanks to MaryEllen with Print Shop Central. Thank you for always going above and beyond.

Foreword

❧

Passion. Grace. Warrior. These three descriptive words describe my wife, Stephenie. As you read this book, let the passion of God's love for you wash over you and make you a warrior for Christ. It doesn't matter what you have done in your past, His grace is sufficient. Let Him make you the warrior you were called to be.

I'm thankful my wife, whom I call "Luvie", continues to allow God to use her to minister through her to others.

– Asbel Montes
Managing Partner at Solutions Group Consulting

❧

I can say from my own personal experience that God did indeed use Stephenie's life and testimony to bring awareness that pain can be transformed to power.

Stephanie presents this valuable teaching about women in the Bible in a way that is both empowering and liberating.

With her servant's heart, Stephanie offers an invitation to women everywhere, who are seeking the Lord's wisdom, intervention, and guidance. We can discover a path that will lead us to the truth, the way, and the life that promises rest for hungering souls. To pursue dream and goals that God has ordained for us, to challenge us to greater heights and wider discovery.

Read it, glean from it and be transformed by it.

– Vani Marshall MS, BCPPC
Counselor and Professor of Psychology

Preface

During the 2020 pandemic that swept the world, I felt the familiar nudge from the Holy Spirit impressing me to write a book about being fearless. But the human side of me stepped in and told God I could not do it because I didn't feel fearless; instead, I felt fear, uncertainty, anxiety, and insecurity at the future for myself, my family, America, and the world. But the nudging of God's Spirit continued to push me, so I eventually opened my heart and began to pour out what had been stirring in my soul. Everyone has something he or she fears or has feared in life. We feel, we hurt, and we do experience fear sometimes, but it doesn't mean that we stop dreaming, praying, and believing. While writing this book, I have come under spiritual attack, have had to dig my heels into much prayer and the Word of God, and have had to be vigilant about keeping the wrong voices out of my life. Come hell or high water, I refuse to allow my mind to become a dumping place for negativity. Instead I am rising with the intent to speak faith, life, and hope into the atmosphere because Jesus is bigger than the chaos that is going on in this world!

Dedication

I dedicate this book to my mother, Joy Haney, who has taught me how to look fear in the eye and to face it with boldness. She has been a woman of great faith for decades and has shown my siblings and me, along with thousands and perhaps millions of other people, what it means to have faith when everything seems hopeless. She has taught me how to pray, read the Bible, and speak faith into a situation that is out of control. I recall an event that happened to her when I was seventeen years old. She had a growth under her chin, and it began to grow until it became the size of a large lemon. You could see this huge lump underneath her chin; it basically stared you straight in the face. Her physician then, Dr. Westifer wanted to do a biopsy and surgery, but Mom refused. You see, during this time, Mom had been leading a group of women at the church in prayer. They would pray for hours upon hours during the morning, and the gathering soon took on an environment like the Book of Acts. Miracles started happening, deliverances occurred, restoration manifested, the gifts of the Spirit were in motion, and the power began to spread. What started as a little prayer meeting turned into a hospital for the sick and a place of refuge for the broken. The city, surrounding communities, and people around the country began to hear about it and started bringing sick loved ones, desperate needs, and their prayer requests to these ladies. They had cancer patients come in, they had terminal patients come in, they had demon-possessed people come in for deliverance, and others would come in for prayer just because they were desperate to see a loved one saved.

The place was busy, the women were bold with their faith, and I watched God do miraculous things. So needless to say, my mother was on fire and full of the Holy Ghost. She was fearless! She was a radical woman on a mission! I will never forget how she would speak to things and they would leave, and I saw cancer patients healed completely. I saw demon-possessed people completely delivered. You can never convince me that this does not happen because I witnessed it with my own eyes. While my mom had this big, ugly lump growing under her chin, she began to pray it away. She told Dr. Westifer that she was going to be healed. He knew my mother was a woman of faith, and he probably thought, *What a radical woman she is!*

I remember vividly as Mom came home, and instead of fearing and speaking doubt, she began to say, "I command you, growth, to go back to hell where you came from," and, "Leave my body in Jesus' name!"

I questioned her and explained, "Mom, it's still there."

But she would answer, "No, it's gone in Jesus' name!"

I also recall when a lady in the church asked her, "Isn't that lying because it's still visible?"

However, my mom replied, "It's gone in Jesus' name!" She took Romans 4:17, "God, who gives life to the dead and calls those things which do not exist as though they did," and applied it to her own life, speaking life and healing into herself.

I can tell you that as a late teenager, I was dealing with a wave of different emotions as I watched my mother having to deal with this large growth under her chin. I thought at times that she was not being practical, and at other times I would get fearful and wonder if it was cancer. If so, what would happen to Mom? Then I would tell myself,

"Mom really is a radical, crazy woman of God!" These are some of the thoughts that cycled through my mind during this time.

My sisters and I sometimes talk about Mom's radical faith and prayer life, for she's influenced us all. We reminisce about some of the miracle stories that we saw while growing up. Mom took Mark 11:22-23 seriously: "And Jesus answering saith unto them, Have faith in God. For verily I say unto you, That whosoever shall say unto this mountain, Be thou removed, and be thou cast into the sea; and shall not doubt in his heart, but shall believe that those things which he saith shall come to pass; he shall have whatsoever he saith" (KJV). While combing her hair or driving, she would curse that growth and tell it to dry up and be removed in Jesus' name! She literally obeyed Mark 11:22-23 and did what Jesus said to do! I would watch her and hear her say pretty much daily, "Leave my body. You have no place here; get out in Jesus' name."

Well, six months later it disappeared completely! Dr. Westifer put in her folder, "Something miraculous has taken place." No one could deny it. I saw God do a miracle in my mother's body, but I also saw a woman who refused to cower in fear or to give up.

Now, I know this is not how everybody's story ends, but regardless of how the story ends, I long to be a fearless woman like my mama. If I'm going down, please don't discourage me from believing in a miracle! Let me believe it till the very end!

The Challenge

I pray that this book will not only encourage you and inspire you, but that it will set a fire in your soul and push you to step out of the norm and to be a fearless woman of God. To be fearless, we must change our thinking; to be fearless, we must be women of prayer. To be fearless, we must be women of the Word. To be fearless, we must not take the bait from others. To be fearless, we must not involve ourselves in petty and unwholesome conversations. To be fearless, we must continue to walk the path of faith even when we feel our faith is wavering. To be fearless, we must stand up to fear and not allow it to cripple our faith!

By the end of this book, you will have been given tools on how to defeat the spirit of fear that is roaming this earth. You will no longer look at fear in the same way. To be fearless means that you don't conform to the norm. To be fearless means that you will have to set aside your preconceived ideas that have been controlling your every move. Oftentimes, we limit ourselves because we allow fear to blur our vision and to get our eyes off the nature of God. A fearless woman of God is willing to jump in all the way with Jesus and will have no regrets doing it.

Table of Contents

THE FEARLESS Woman

by STEPHENIE HANEY-MONTES

CHAPTER 1

The Vigilant Woman

Your mind is on the enemy's hit list, so you must be vigilant against every negative and toxic thought that tries to come in and take up residence inside your mind.

A s we dive into this first chapter to discuss the battle in the mind, I want to give you the actual definition of *fearless*. The dictionary defines *fearless* as: "To be free from fear and to be brave." But let's go ahead and tackle the elephant in the room before we move any further. To be a fearless woman of God does not mean that your life will always be completely free from fear. Every person regardless of age, gender, or culture has struggled with fear in his or her life, and we will continue to stare fear in the face more often than not because we are human to the core.

Throughout the Bible though we are told to not fear and are reminded that we must put our trust in the One and only, Jesus Christ. "For I, the LORD your God, will hold your right hand, Saying to you, 'Fear not, I will help you' " (Isaiah 41:13). Jesus knew that we would struggle with fear, but thankfully, we can look to the Scriptures that tell us to not fear and that remind us He is with us through every trial, storm, setback, and difficulty we face in life. Now, I must insert a disclaimer right here and tell you that I have had my share of fears and doubts. Speaking faith hasn't always come easy for me. Sometimes speaking life gets lost in my muddled thoughts, and sometimes

I am just plain tired of fighting the good fight of faith. Sometimes I don't want to put on a brave face; sometimes I don't want to act like everything is fine when it's not fine. Sometimes I don't feel like showing up, but sometimes I just want to crawl into a quiet place from the world and hide. Yeah, sometimes that's my reality, but it never seems to fail that no matter what type of battle I find myself in, there always seems to be what I call "bulldog grit." It shakes me and says, "Stephenie, you can do this! It's not time to quit!" I will then pick myself up, go into full throttle again, and continue to fight the good fight of faith. If you're going to be a fearless woman of God, you are going to have to prepare yourself for the battle. Instead of shrinking into the shadows and throwing your calling into the trash, you have to get some "bulldog grit" inside your soul, and no matter what comes your way, determine within yourself that you are going to be a fearless woman of God.

In the Beginning

In the Book of Genesis, Adam and Eve could not even comprehend what the word "fear" meant. They had never experienced that feeling of fear that comes suddenly, oftentimes like a cup of hot liquid has just been poured over your entire body, and makes the hairs on the back of your neck stand up. If the feeling of fear continues, anxiety usually will step in and cause your heart rate to go up, and it can even paralyze you mentally and stop you from moving forward. When fear hits us, it takes over our entire thought process, which in return affects our physical being. You who have dealt with anxiety or panic attacks understand this scenario well.

In Genesis 2, God told Adam and Eve that they could eat everything in the garden. There was only one tree from which they could not eat, the tree of knowledge of good and evil. "And the Lord God commanded the man, saying, "Of every tree of the garden you may freely eat; 17 but of the tree of the knowledge of good and evil you shall not eat, for in the day that you eat of it you shall surely die." (Genesis 2:16-17).

Think about that. They could eat anything in the garden but were told that only one tree was off limits. What happened? Well, that invisible enemy is always prowling about, trying to trip us up, and that is what he did to Adam and Eve. He tripped them up and caused them to mess up the flow of the life God had created for them. In Genesis 3 the serpent did not approach Adam first, but he actually approached Eve instead. My mother has always said, "The woman has a lot of power in her marriage and relationships. The man is the head, but the woman is the neck. She can turn his head for good, or she can turn his head for bad." The serpent for some reason sought Eve first instead of Adam. Off the record, I think the serpent was confident he could convince Eve to do exactly what he wanted her to do. If he could turn Eve's heart, Adam would follow her lead. Ladies, you have more power than you give yourself credit for, so use it wisely.

Satan was able to get inside Eve's head, and from there things began to spiral downward. He began to use his professional schemes on her, throwing his charming self in the mix, he was able to seduce her heart, and then he had her hooked. Sadly, he would win this round and would tempt her to concede and to go totally against what God had told both her and Adam not to do.

"Then the serpent said to the woman, "You will not surely die. For God knows that in the day you eat of it your eyes will be opened, and you will be like God, knowing good and evil" (Genesis 3:4-5). He was playing on her vulnerability. He was trying to find a weakness in her resolve, and in verses 6 and 7, we see that he found that place and was able to get inside her head. "So when the woman saw that the tree was good for food, that it was pleasant to the eyes, and a tree desirable to make one wise, she took of its fruit and ate. She also gave to her husband with her, and he ate. Then the eyes of both of them were opened, and they knew that they were naked; and they sewed fig leaves together and made themselves coverings."

By Eve's giving into the enemy, she wrecked her and Adam's fairytale lifestyle. Everything had been going so good for them; they had what we would call the perfect life. They had everything anybody could ever hope for, but now they were going to experience pain and fear. The honeymoon stage was over. If you move down to Genesis 3:9-13, you learn the outcome.

Then the LORD God called to Adam and said to him, "Where are you?" So he said, "I heard Your voice in the garden, and I was afraid because I was naked; and I hid myself." And He said, "Who told you that you were naked? Have you eaten from the tree of which I commanded you that you should not eat?" Then the man said, "The woman whom You gave to be with me, she gave me of the tree, and I ate." And the LORD God said to the woman, "What is this you have done?" The woman said, "The serpent deceived me, and I ate."

In verse 10, Adam voiced the famous saying that we often hear in the world today, "I was afraid." Fear was now going to be a part of their lives forever; their future would never include a period without this emotion. They would always battle with the fear that so many deal with nowadays. How many times have we said, "I was afraid," "I am afraid," "I fear what is going on," or "I feel kind of fearful about the future"? We express how we feel about fear in many different ways, but we can all agree that fear comes to us all. Since that day when Adam and Eve ate the forbidden fruit, fear has become a common denominator in the lives of humans, and it roams the earth, never taking a break.

The serpent was able to get inside Eve's mind. I would love to talk to Eve face to face, to ask her what went through her mind when she felt herself weakening and giving in to the enemy's ruse. What exact word did the serpent say to her that convinced her? Was it the tone of his voice? Was it the look he gave her? What caused her to second-guess God? When was the exact moment she gave in? Could she not even consult with God about it first? After all, He is the One who created her and Adam, and she wouldn't even be alive had it not been for the Almighty. I would think that He would be the safe place to which they could run. I would think that she would look to God before she made any decisions in her life. But as we read their story, it becomes apparent that the serpent was extremely charming and that Eve was not able to discern right from wrong. He obviously was able to pull the blinders over her eyes so much that she could not see who he really was. The other thing it lets me know is that we as women of God must be vigilant about protecting our minds, our homes, our marriages, and our relationships along with the calling that God has placed on our lives.

Now isn't the time to become enamored with a snake (a person) who is saying all the right things even though your gut is telling you that something is off, nor is it the time to throw yourself into the arms of a person from whom your internal radar tells you to run. But now is the time to discern your surroundings and to know what and whom you are allowing into that place that you call safe. I often say, "Don't let your mind be someone else's garbage can." In other words, don't allow just anyone to dump his or her junk into your mind and to pour toxicity into you. Oftentimes if we are not careful, we will become acclimated to a toxic person without even realizing it because we have become too familiar with that voice. That is what happened with Eve. "And the woman said to the serpent, 'We may eat the fruit of the trees of the garden; but of the fruit of the tree which is in the midst of the garden, God has said, "You shall not eat it, nor shall you touch it, lest you die' " (Genesis 3:2-3). Notice in this passage of Scripture that she was clear about where she stood. At that point, you can tell that Eve was not going to allow anything to come in or to tempt her to compromise on what the Lord had told her and Adam in the beginning. She told the serpent that God said they could not eat from that particular tree, and that should have been the end of the conversation. She should have excused herself right then and there, found Adam, and said, "We have a problem. The serpent is trying to destroy us. He wants us to disobey God. He is quite the charmer, has a seducing tongue, and speaks eloquently, but my spiritual intuition has tapped in and has told me to run from him."

But once she allowed the serpent to continue the conversation, something in his voice—whether it was his charm, wit, or charisma—sold her, and he was able to convince her that she didn't have to listen to the voice of God. He persuaded her she would be fine doing it her own way. That is when she gave in, and then she went to her husband and was able to influence him also to disobey what the Lord had told them not to do.

I want to park here for a moment to say, "Dear _____ (fill in your name), you can use your influence for good, or you can use it for bad. We all have a choice."

Adam and Eve went from having no fear to experiencing fear, all because Eve had allowed a toxic and slimy voice to get inside her head. The mind is the location of our hardest battle! In the mind we battle fear, but there we also decide whether or not we are going to coddle it or get rid of it. We have to protect the mind as if our life depends on it, for it most definitely will determine where you will end up. But the good thing is that, when we do have these anxious feelings of fear come to sneak in and try to take up residence inside our minds, we can immediately turn to Jesus. We can nip it without even entertaining it. "Be strong and courageous, do not be afraid or tremble in dread before them, for it is the Lord your God who goes with you. He will not fail you or abandon you" (Deuteronomy 31:6). In other versions, the last part of the verse says, "He will never leave you nor forsake you."

Even when your thoughts are scattered and your mind is struggling to make the right decision, just know that God will never leave you nor forsake you and that He can help you to make the right decisions in life. The Word of God can help calm our restless hearts and still our thoughts so that, even in the midst of circumstances outside our control, we can still feel the peace of God in our lives. But this requires critical thinking, as in changing our thought patterns to focus on the Word of God first instead of using it as a last resort. Oftentimes we try to fix the issue on our own, but when it begins to spiral out of control, we turn to Jesus in desperation. I challenge you to turn to the Scriptures first to guide your thoughts and to keep you in perfect peace. "You will keep him in perfect peace, whose mind is stayed on You, because He trusts in You" (Isaiah 26:3). We must keep our thoughts on the bigger picture, which is Jesus Christ and His plan for our lives. It's imperative that you take time to read the Word of God and to allow the Scriptures to be the driving force in your life. When you are feeling fragile and vulnerable and your mind is under attack, don't go into battle on your own; instead lean on the Word, prayer, and Jesus. Allow Him to guide you and to show you what to do.

Protect Your Mind

As we think, we change the physical nature of our brain.
As we consciously direct our thinking, we can wipe out toxic patterns of thinking and replace them with healthy thoughts.

– Dr. Caroline Leaf

The biggest battle we all face is between our two ears. It's called the mind!

Have you ever felt extremely confident in moving forward with a new job, new life, new everything? You felt as if nothing could come in and take you down from the "cloud nine" feeling you were on. Perhaps you bought a brand-new car, maybe even a brand-new home, or you got a new make-over with your attire and home and felt ecstatic about your life. Maybe you have an awesome boyfriend or husband, your career is thriving, and your ministry is exceeding all of your expectations. You are now flying high like an eagle. You are in a state of mind where you feel fearless and determined to plow through anything that tries to get in the way. It's a wonderful feeling of exhilaration. But let's be honest here. That incredible feeling of exhilaration can be interrupted at any moment if, all of a sudden, the tide shifts.

The choppy waves of life can turn toward you and try to drown you with heartache, frustration, and disappointment. Oftentimes when we are in the middle of a vicious storm, we will try to make sense of what is going on as we deal with the nagging little voice of fear that tries to worm its way into our minds. You may be in a place this very moment where you feel disconcerted, trying desperately to keep your head above water. Basically, you're just trying to survive. But allow me to iterate this, "To be fearless doesn't mean that you will never experience fear." It does not mean that you will never have your doubts, nor does not it mean that you will never feel like throwing in the towel. It means, in spite of the horrific curveballs being thrown at you, that you are still going to pick yourself back up physically, emotionally, and spiritually and are going to refuse to go down without a fight!

The Mind
It's where everything goes.
It's where everything we hear and listen to is stored.
It's where we make decisions.
It's where we make assumptions.
It's where we refuse to listen to negativity, or it's where we welcome negativity.
It's where we struggle with the whys in life.
It's where depression sets in.
It's where happiness begins.
It's where anxiety steps in.
It's where peace steps in.
It's where fear steps in.
It's where we decide whether we will give up or will continue to push through the difficulties in life.
It's where the battle lies; therefore, we must be vigilant with protecting it.

Repeat after me, "The battle is in the mind!" If you really want to get on the right path to becoming fearless, you will need to re-shape your thinking and change your mindset. The mind can keep us from achieving great things in life and from doing great things for the kingdom of God. I sometimes cannot even wrap my head around how tiny the brain is while at the same time recognizing just how powerful that tiny thing is. Most scientists will agree that the average adult human brain weighs around three pounds, yet it controls everything we say and do. So we must continue to combat the unhealthy things that come to our mind, try to linger, and attempt to mess with our faith. Satan will toy with your thoughts and distract you from what God is trying to do in your life. It's a mind game with him, for He wants to destroy what God is doing in you! He goes after the mind because the mind can be vulnerable, but when we are vigilant about protecting it, we will think on the things of God and on things above. Colossians 3:2 tells us, "Set your mind on things above, not on things on the earth." Don't allow the enemy to distort what God has called you to do! Don't allow the enemy to tell you that you were not delivered and that you will never over-come the past! Don't allow the enemy to tell you that you will be sick for the rest of your life! Don't allow the enemy to tell you that you will never become free from depression! Step up to the plate, and protect your mind!

We are attacked in our minds by many things. These can cause us to put the word "fearless" on the back burner because we convince ourselves there is no way we can be fearless while we are dealing with these different emotions.

Here are a few things that always seem to get in the way. Unfortunately, they often come when we are feeling somewhat vulnerable.

- *Fear* - is like a beast with no mercy. It will take over your entire life if you allow it to. It will consume your mind if you allow it to. We sometimes need to remind ourselves that the name of Jesus is more powerful than the fear in this world. John Newton said, "How sweet the name of Jesus sounds in a believer's ear! It soothes his sorrows, heals his wounds, and drives away his fear." The Word of God is also more powerful than fear, so we must replace the fear that tries to take up space in our mind with the Word of God. Quote the Scriptures over your mind and your situation. Isaiah 41:10 says, "Fear not, for I am with you; Be not dismayed, for I am your God. I will strengthen you, Yes, I will help you, I will uphold you with My righteous right hand." No matter what we face in life, God tells us (AMP), "Do not fear [anything], for I am with you; Do not be afraid, for I am your God. I will strengthen you, be assured I will help you; I will certainly take hold of you with My righteous right hand [a hand of justice, of power, of victory, of salvation]."

- *Worry* - keeps us up at night, can bring on bouts of anxiety, and can take our focus off what God is doing. The definition for *worry* is "a way to anxiety or unease; allow one's mind to dwell on difficulty or trouble." Corrie Ten Boom said, "Worry does not empty tomorrow of its sorrow, it empties today of its strength. "When I am afraid, I will put my trust and faith in You" (Psalm 56:3). And 1 Peter 5:7 tells us, "Casting all your cares [all your anxieties, all your worries, and all your concerns, once and for all] on Him, for He cares about you [with deepest affection, and watches over you very carefully]." When worry tries to tear down the door that is connected to your mind, you need to put your faith and trust in God and to cast all your cares upon Him.

- *Doubt* - will sometimes sneak in and take over without our even realizing it. "Immediately the father of the child cried out and said with tears, "Lord, I believe; help my unbelief!" (Mark 9:24). The man struggled with doubt since his son had been possessed with a spirit for a long time. I'm sure he was thinking, *We have been in this season so long that I just don't know if we will ever become free from it.* He was focused more on the demonic spirit than on the miracle that was coming, but he knew there was something different about Jesus and cried to Him, "Lord, help my unbelief." This story resonates with all of us because we all know what it's like to struggle with our feelings and doubts. But we don't have to stay there; we can rise and say, "Father, help my unbelief. Jesus, I am struggling with doubt today."

- *Depression* – may try to take over your mind, but remember that you are not alone and that you can become free from it. We can't see depression on the outside, yet it's affecting millions of people around the world. It will try to cripple your faith, will push you into a dark place, and will cause you to think things that are not good for your soul. I have been there, so I know the effects it has on the mind. The Word of God became a stable place for me during that dark season. Here are a few verses to speak over your mind when you are struggling with depression:

- "But You, O LORD, are a shield for me, My glory and the One who lifts up my head" (Psalm 3:3).

"The thief does not come except to steal, and to kill, and to destroy. I have come that they may have life, and that they may have it more abundantly" (John 10:10).

"You have turned for me my mourning into dancing; You have put off my sackcloth and clothed me with gladness" (Psalm 30:11).

- ***The Past*** - has a reputation for trying to convince you that you cannot fulfill your purpose because you have too much baggage hanging over your life. It will also try to tell you that you are not qualified to do what God is calling you to do. But it's high time that you respond with confidence and say, "You are not going to control me anymore! I'm done with you!"

Not that I have already obtained it [this goal of being Christ-like], or have already been made perfect, but I actively press on so that I may take hold of that [perfection] for which Christ Jesus took hold of me and made me His own. Brothers and sisters, I do not consider that I have made it my own yet; but one thing I do: forgetting what lies behind and reaching forward to what lies ahead, I press on toward the goal to win the [heavenly] prize of the upward call of God in Christ Jesus (Philippians 3:12-14).

- ***Confusion*** – comes in as the enemy tries to confuse you about the direction you need to go. He will do this through your thoughts, assumptions, and questions and will also use people to bring confusion into your life. Make sure that those from whom you are receiving advice are in sync with what God is doing in your life. "Trust in the LORD with all your heart, And lean not on your own understanding; In all your ways acknowledge him, And he shall direct your paths" (Proverbs 3:5-6).

You are what you feed your mind.

Not too long ago, while we were in the middle of the COVID-19 pandemic, my husband was recording a clip to share with his friends on social media. He was telling them to turn the news off and to focus on good things because it wasn't healthy for them to fill their minds constantly with things that caused them to feel fear and anxiety. He asked my opinion while he was recording it, and I chimed in and said, "You are what you feed your mind." That means if I listen to negativity all day long, I'm going to start speaking negativity all day long. If I listen to positive things, read the Word of God, stay prayerful, and focus on God things, I'm going to speak faith, life, and hope. My parents instilled the mantra, "You are what you feed your mind," into me at a young age. I've tried to follow that piece of advice for the most part, but I must confess that I have failed miserably a few times and have found myself spewing negativity and joining ranks with Chicken Little in saying, "The sky is falling." My tongue was busy flapping, speaking unwholesome things into the atmosphere because of what I had allowed to pour into me.

I'm quite the stickler now on what and whom I allow to pour into me. It's definitely become more personal for me since I now have some experience with how the enemy attacks. It's finally sunk in, that what I allow my mind to think on is what will shape me and my future. If I listen to negativity all day, guess what? I'm going to start regurgitating negativity all day. If I have friends who are always talking about people or giving me the latest scoop on someone's mistakes and failures, I too am going to become more critical of other people's lives. If I allow myself to entertain the news constantly, live 24/7 on social media, and allow my mind to view and hear things that are not uplifting, those venues will affect me whether or not I think they will. Why? Because you are what you feed your mind. If I allow my thoughts to run carelessly, I am going to get into trouble. As the old saying goes, "An idle mind is the devil's playground." Not everyone is being vigilant about protecting his or her mind. If we all were careful in this regard, we wouldn't be in the current frenzy and mess we are experiencing. The mind is the enemy's playground, and if you give him an opening, he's going to take it and will end up wreaking havoc in your life. We must let the words of our mouth and the meditation of our hearts be acceptable in the sight of the Lord.

Let the words of my mouth and the meditation of my heart
Be acceptable in Your sight, O LORD,
my strength and my Redeemer (Psalm 19:14).

Change your Mindset

Depending on what they are, our habits will either make us or break us. We become what we repeatedly do.

– Sean Covey

If you are battling negative thoughts and feel like you need to do a complete turnaround, the Word gives clear direction on how to do it. "Don't copy the behavior and customs of this world, but let God transform you into a new person by changing the way you think. Then you will learn to know God's will for you, which is good and pleasing and perfect" (Romans 12:2, New Living Translation).

Let's break this verse down.

1. **"Don't copy the world's behavior."** We should never allow the system of the world to dictate to us how we should react, respond, and talk. The world's behaviors and customs are completely opposite of God's nature. We must be vigilant against this mentality that has made its way into the church.

2. **"Let God transform you [your mind]"** means: let Him completely change your way of thinking. This isn't always easy to do, so you will have to be intentional about it because the influence of the world is everywhere. Unfortunately, many Christians have allowed it to enter into their lives.

3. **"Which is good and pleasing and perfect."** When God transforms our thinking, it will be in sync with His thinking. This is why we must plug into His way of thinking always and stop utilizing the world's way of thinking. Let's not repeat the narrative of the world but let us repeat the narrative of Jesus Christ.

You cannot be talking out of both sides of your mouth if you expect to be a fearless woman of God. You will have to take extreme measures and put some serious boundaries in place if you expect to take the step of faith and to walk fearlessly through the season you are in. If you don't, you will experience a yo-yo mindset and way of life. You will be positive and upbeat one day, and then the next day you will find yourself in the depths of despair. You cannot ride the fence and expect to have a sound mind. You have to choose sides.

Either you are going all the way with God, or you are going to cross to the other side and follow the world's behaviors and customs. You can't do both. If you try to straddle the fence, you will be a miserable wreck and always on edge.

The mind affects your speech.

The hardships we deal with in life will play with our thoughts and emotions and will sometimes even cause us to question God and His plan. They will also cause you to say things that you should not say. My mother has a quote in her book, *Power of Speaking Positive,* "The mouth is the mirror of the mind, heart, and soul." How right she is! The tongue often reveals what is happening inside a person. This is why studying the Word, meditating on it, getting it deep into your heart, and speaking it into the atmosphere around you are imperative. When we get the Word in our hearts, it will help our tongue to talk right, and we will not be so quick to speak things that are contrary to the Word of God. Protect your mind with the Word of God! Use the Word of God to fight the negative thoughts that try to discourage you! Look to the Word of God to help you to change your mindset so that you can start living victoriously! Be vigilant against the voices in this world that try to contaminate your mind. It's not time to take a back seat. It's time to be on the front lines, and it's time to protect your mind at all costs.

We need to apply the following passages of Scripture to our lives on a daily basis. This will help us to keep our tongues from wagging and from saying things we should not say.

"Death and life are in the power of the tongue"
(Proverbs 18:21).

The Message says, "Words kill, words give life; they're either poison or fruit—you choose."

"Do not let unwholesome [foul, profane, worthless, vulgar] words ever come out of your mouth, but only such speech as is good for building up others, according to the need and the occasion, so that it will be a blessing to those who hear [you speak]" (Ephesians 4:29).

"Indeed, we put bits in horses' mouths that they may obey us, and we turn their whole body. Look also at ships: although they are so large and are driven by fierce winds, they are turned by a very small rudder wherever the pilot desires. Even so the tongue is a little member and boasts great things. See how great a forest a little fire kindles! And the tongue is a fire, a world of iniquity. The tongue is so set among our members that it defiles the whole body, and sets on fire the course of nature; and it is set on fire by hell" (James 3:3-6).

"Out of the same mouth proceed blessing and cursing. My brethren, these things ought not to be so" (James 3:10).

"He who would love life And see good days, Let him refrain his tongue from evil, And his lips from speaking deceit" (1 Peter 3:10).

If you want to speak right, you have to think right. Everything starts in the mind. Our words reveal what is going on in the heart, mind, and soul, so you must remain vigilant with what you are feeding your mind.

It's not always going to be a smooth ride.

In order to be fearless and in order to change your mindset so that you can be more in sync with God's ways, you will need to set aside the idea that it's going to be a smooth ride while you gallop away into doing your God assignments. It's going to be a ride, yes, but it's not always going to be a smooth ride. Your calling, courage, bravery, and commitment will be challenged by the enemy. When this happens, you need to determine in your heart that with God on your side, you can face the adversary who has been trying to torment you. You can face anything that tries to darken the door of your heart and home, so don't give in and cower to the fear tactics that come from the enemy.

"Though an army encamp against me, My heart shall not fear; Though war may rise against me, In this I will be confident" (Psalm 27:3). David penned this psalm during a difficult time when all his enemies pursued him. I love his phrase, "My heart shall not fear." We all know that David struggled with fear, anxiety, and bouts of depression, but here he spoke faith into the atmosphere. Then he went on to say, "Though war may rise against me, In this I will be confident." He was basically saying, "I'm in a tough spot and this isn't easy for me, but my heart shall not fear. I will remain confident." Like David, you must speak faith into the atmosphere, and even when you struggle with your own emotions and unhealthy thoughts, don't stop speaking faith, life, and hope over yourself!

To change the direction of your life, you first need to change your mindset.

We are all guilty of holding on to things that give us a false feeling of comfort. "But test all things carefully [so you can recognize what is good]. Hold firmly to that which is good" (1 Thessalonians 5:21). If you truly want to change your thought patterns, you are going to have to let go of some things.

You will have to let go of:

1. *Your personal agenda.* You've planned out this whole year to a T, but God wants to take your pen to write His vision for your life. It's time to put the pen down and to allow God

to lead you to those places to which He is calling you to go. "We can make our plans, but the LORD determines our steps" (Proverbs 16:9, *New Living Translation*).

2. ***The way you've always done things.*** What if God is wanting to do something different this time? Can you let go and let God take you to the garden of Gethsemane to teach you some new things that will blow your mind and stretch your faith? Sometimes you need to look straight ahead and not look to the right nor to the left to avoid being distracted from what God is doing in your life. "Let your eyes look straight ahead, And your eyelids look right before you" (Proverbs 4:25).

3. ***Relationships that have been holding you back.*** There comes a time in your life when you need to cut some things loose and not allow toxicity to get inside of your mind anymore. "Become wise by walking with the wise; hang out with fools and watch your life fall to pieces" (Proverbs 13:20, *The Message*).

4. ***Wrong voices.*** Remove the wrong voices from your life that are not meant to go where God is taking you. Ask Him to help you to differentiate between the right and wrong voices in your life. The enemy will use anything and anyone to come into your life to try to mess up your thinking. "But the Lord is faithful, who will establish you and guard you from the evil one" (2 Thessalonians 3:3).

These things are going to affect your mind one way or the other, so it's important for all of us to do some inward inventory and figure out what needs tweaking. Sometimes we get stuck in a funk and use the saying, "This is how I've always done it." Well, maybe it's time to hit the reset button and to change things up a bit. Start with a clean slate.

In order to do this, you must completely change your way of thinking. When we recondition our mindset, we change our habits, our ways, and our lives. But it's not easy trying to break unhealthy habits that we have been doing for a long time. I remember as a young lady dealing with a bad breakup and trying to break free from a negative mindset. An enormous amount of unhealthy thoughts inundated me. During this time, I also realized that some of my inner circle were not feeding me the proper diet for my emotional and spiritual health. Their advice and input did not advance me to the front line of freedom but actually pushed me to the bottom of the barrel, where I felt I would never overcome the curveball that had been thrown at me. You will never overcome a past of troubled waters if you do not nip the unhealthy thoughts that have taken over your mind.

The mind can become fragile when we experience grief due to a death, divorce, or estranged relationship. It can also become weary of the battle, the storms, and the fiery trials we deal with in life. Life in general can exhaust us to the point where we feel we just can't go on. This is when we must be intentional about protecting our minds. At this moment we must purpose in our hearts that we will change our mindset from focusing on the negative to focusing on the positive, and then we must catch the vision of the greatness of Jesus. We must seek Him and His strength always. "Seek the LORD and His strength; Seek His face continually [longing to be in His presence]" (1 Chronicles 16:11).

You may not be able to control what happens on the outside, but you can control what happens inside.

You have power over your mind—not outside events.
Realize this and you will find strength.

– Marcus Aurelius, Roman emperor 161-180

We cannot always control what goes on around us, but we can control what goes on in our minds. We can overcome, but we must be purposeful about it. Overcomers are followers of Christ, who resist the power and temptation of the world's philosophies that try to steer them from God's truth. Overcoming requires complete dependence upon Jesus Christ for direction, purpose, fulfillment, and strength to follow His plan for our lives. When you find yourself struggling in your thoughts and are tempted to dabble in negativity due to your circumstances, I implore you to trust in the Lord. Isaiah 26:4 (New Living Translation) tells us, "Trust in the LORD always, for the LORD GOD is the eternal Rock." Do not allow the pessimistic voices to cripple your faith! They will come and go, but Jesus remains constant and faithful. "Jesus Christ is the same yesterday, today, and forever" (Hebrews 13:8).

What are you feeding your mind?

Perhaps we all need to ask ourself this question. I'm not talking about literal food although many health experts tell us that the best things for the mind are walnuts, avocados, beets, salmon, and broccoli, just to name a few. I know this because my mother is what we call a "health nut." She juices, she chooses extremely healthy food, and she disciplines herself daily to follow this lifestyle. She has told me more than once to eat one of these food items because it is good for the brain. Of course, when my siblings and I were younger, we didn't take these food suggestions too seriously, but as we've gotten older, we definitely know what we need to eat if we want to be healthy. But discipline is the one ingredient we must have in order to do any of this. Discipline means showing a controlled form of behavior or way of working. We can continue loading up on sugar and junk food, and eventually it's going to catch up with us. Or we can tell ourself that we are changing direction in our diets and are not going to do things the way we've always done them.

I can tell you emphatically that as soon as you begin to do a lifestyle change with your diet and way of life, you need to be prepared for the temptations that will come your way. If you are serious about your health and are focused, it will take a few weeks to get past the stages of craving the junk food you used to consume. In order to break a habit, you will have to push against the temptation that calls you to go back to the way you've always lived. But once you stay the course for a while, you will begin to feel absolutely incredible, and the results will be well worth it.

This is exactly how it is with the mind. We must discipline ourselves so that we can set healthy boundaries with the unhealthy things try to make their way into our thought process.

1. Some things you must discard immediately and refuse to allow them to fester because they are toxic to the soul. There is no tiptoeing around the issue, nor should you try to justify it. In order to truly move on, you must get rid of those things.

2. You need to ask yourself if your boundaries are clear to the other party. It's important for you to be clear and precise with the boundaries you set. When you are not clear, confusion follows. This allows the other party to feel entitled so that he or she will try to manipulate you into doing things you know you should not do.

3. You may be in the middle of a situation that is causing you to feel fear, depression, and anxiety. This is not the time to sit back and to allow these things to take over your life; instead, you need to get some grit and to push through these difficult feelings until you feel some relief.

4. You may be dealing with a sense of hopelessness permeating your thoughts due to your current environment. Many people are in unhealthy spaces and places that affect their mindsets and decisions. It's imperative that you start with baby steps and move forward into making the right decisions that will help you to become free from the dysfunction that has made its way into your personal space.

In order to handle your current situation, you need to be vigilant from here and disciplined enough to set healthy boundaries. It's easy to fall prey to living in a cycle of negativity and toxicity, but you don't have to stay there. If you are serious about changing your mindset, you will begin to tell yourself, "I'm not filling my mind with this," or "I don't have to sit here and listen to this," or "I'm not allowing this to consume me anymore." Then excuse yourself and walk away. If you are serious about protecting your mind, you must take the initiative and break the cycle of dysfunction and negativity. Paul explained in 1 Corinthians 9:27, "But I discipline my body and bring it into subjection, lest, when I have preached to others, I myself should become disqualified." The Message translates this, "I don't know about you, but I'm running hard for the finish line. I'm giving it everything I've got. No lazy living for me! I'm staying alert and in top condition. I'm not going to get caught napping, telling everyone else all about it and then missing out myself." Paul knew how important it was to discipline the body (the mind). He is a great example for us, for he disciplined his thoughts, his habits, and his speech. He ran a hard race all the way to the finish line and gave it everything he had, and so can we.

Resist the Enemy

Growing up I would often hear my parents say, "If the enemy can get you in the mind, he's got you. You must resist the enemy." They were stating, "You better get a grip on your thoughts, you better get some spunk in your spine, and stop allowing the enemy to play mind games with you." I learned at an early age that to resist Satan is a good thing. I've also learned that as a woman of God I am fully capable of being able to stand my ground against every arrow that comes my way because the power that is within me is greater than the enemy who seeks to destroy my soul. "You are of God, little children, and have overcome them, because He who is in you is greater than he who is in the world" (1 John 4:4). Paul told us in 1 Corinthians 2:5 that our faith must rest in the power of God alone. "That your faith should not be in the wisdom of men but in the power of God." As women of God, we don't need an entourage to carry us through the battle in the mind, but if we are full of the Holy Ghost, we can and we will speak with authority and boldness when we need to address the enemy.

Will Reagan wrote a song that has challenged me to keep the fire burning in my soul.

Set a fire down in my soul
That I can't contain and I can't control
I want more of You, God.
I want more of You, God.

Having a fire in our soul gives us the gumption to be vigilant about protecting our minds. Having a fire in our soul helps us to graduate from being apathetic women who just exist to becoming passionate women for the kingdom of God.

I must admit that at a young age I didn't fully grasp what my parents' words, "If the enemy can get in your mind, he's got you." But as I've gotten older, I definitely have grasped this solidly. If given the chance, I would scream from the mountaintops to every woman fighting the good fight of faith, "Protect your mind! Don't give the enemy—or just anybody, for that matter—a way into your thoughts. Be vigilant!" After going through some horrific trials in my life, I can tell you without reservation that I'm not wasting any more of my precious time playing games with the adversary, but I'm being intentional about resisting everything he throws my way.

Here are a few things that will mess with your mind and cause you to become consumed with the negativity in the world.

1. The news outlets . . . Be informed, not consumed.

2. Negative people, including some friends . . . Don't allow someone else's anger and chaos to become yours.

3. Noise . . . The noise in this world constantly throws out lies, assumptions, and opinions. Be careful what you believe, and always look to the Word of God for guidance and clarity.

4. Voices . . . The voices that spew fear-mongering narratives are contrary to the Word of God. Don't allow the fear talk, which some are annoyingly pontificating, to get inside your spirit.

If we don't resist the ploys of the enemy, he is going to push his agenda into our personal spaces. If this happens, we should not be surprised when we feel anxious, fearful, and chaotic.

James 4:7 tells us, "Therefore submit to God. Resist the devil and he will flee from you." To resist something is to keep it at bay or to fend off its influence or advance. This is what we have to do as Christian women; we must fend off the influence of the enemy. But first, we must submit to God because that is what the Scripture says. Submit, and then resist the devil. If we follow this order, the Bible gives us the promise that the devil will flee. If you do not heed James 4:7, you take the risk of allowing the enemy to play inside your mind, which in return will put you on an emotional roller-coaster ride while you believe his lies. We must resist anything and everything that goes against the Word of God. We must protect our minds and change our mindset because the battle is in the mind.

The mind is powerful! Our thoughts are powerful! We cannot stop random ideas from entering our minds, but we can control how we entertain the negative thoughts that come to us. It's been said by experts that the mind produces sixty thousand to eighty thousand thoughts a day. That's an average of twenty-five hundred to thirty-three hundred thoughts per hour, a pretty incredible statistic. Other experts estimate a smaller number of fifty thousand thoughts per day, about twenty-one hundred thoughts per hour. So according to the experts, we have thousands of thoughts running through our minds on a daily basis. What are we doing with them? How are we utilizing them? The first line of Proverbs 23:7 counsels, "For as he thinks in his heart, so is he." Do you feel trapped inside your mind with racing thoughts that are not healthy? Some of you are in the thick of the battle right now, and you feel a little rattled with your thinking. Your thought process is out of sorts. Maybe your thoughts have taken over your life and have created a sense of hopelessness. We all face difficulties that cause us to feel this way sometimes, but we must not allow the sensation to linger too long. Every child of God is going to come face to face with an attack on the mind, but with God's strength we can face it, address it, and not allow it to define who we are. "That He would grant you, according to the riches of His glory, to be strengthened with might through His Spirit in the inner man" (Ephesians 3:16).

We can do the following to resist those nagging toxic and negative thoughts that come to us:

1. **Identify your negative thoughts.** One of the biggest issues we have as humans is that we try to suppress what we really need to be addressing. A few years back I spoke about depression at a conference and was able to reference a finding from the National Institute of Mental Health: at one time 7.1 percent of Americans were suffering with depression. Now, keep in mind that they reached this number based on those who actually reached out for help, but I am sure the numbers were even higher in actuality then and are much higher now because there are many who suffer alone in their thoughts. Why do I know that? Because I too have not always reached out for help for the depression and instead tried to solve the issue on my own. I counsel many who are battling negative thoughts, depression, fear, anxiety, and other extreme disorders and emotions. Ladies, it's a thing, it's happening, and we can't continue to ignore it or to pretend it isn't occurring.

"In the multitude of my anxieties within me, Your comforts delight my soul" (Psalm 94:19).

"The fear of man brings a snare, But whoever trusts in *and* puts his confidence in the Lord will be exalted *and* safe."
(Proverbs 29:25)

When we struggle with our thoughts, we also need to read Scriptures that speak life into us. For some, you cannot allow yourself to let your thoughts go into those dark places because then suicidal thoughts will come. For others, you have been dealing with depression for a while as you feel blah, have no drive, weep all the time, and have no energy to deal with your battle. Others have an off-and-on "in the funk" feeling, but it still affects your mindset and gets in the way of your productivity in anything that you attempt to focus on. I cannot stress this enough, but it is imperative that you feed your mind Scriptures that speak life into you, that encourage you, and that remind you that you are not alone and that you will get through this. I encourage those of you who struggle with suicidal thoughts to seek godly professional counseling immediately and to get the help you need. The devil would love to take you down, so beware. Stand guard over your mind. Resist him! Combat every negative thought that knocks on your door.

2. **Write.** Write each thought that has caused you to feel insecure and powerless.

Meditate on Psalm 104:33-34: "I will sing to the LORD as long as I live; I will sing praise to my God while I have my being. May my meditation be sweet to Him; I will be glad in the LORD." Oftentimes journaling our thoughts can help us to address the negativity in a more prudent way and can also help us to see the progress we are making as we remain vigilant in combatting the negative thoughts. Do not allow your thoughts to run wild in your mind, but rein them in and remember that God can help you to overcome them.

3. **Pray.** "I surrender my thoughts. I can't do this without You, Lord. I need You to step in and to calm my thoughts. I need You to bring peace to my mind. I need You to restore my faith. I need You to wrap Your arms around me as I walk through this difficult time. You know my thoughts, and You know my heart, O Lord. Deliver me and guide my footsteps."

Psalm 139 is a passage that goes deep into our thoughts, a prayer we all can apply to our lives.

O LORD, *you have searched me and known me.*
2 You know my sitting down and my rising up;
You understand my thought afar off.
3 You comprehend my path and my lying down,
And are acquainted with all my ways.
4 For there is not a word on my tongue
But behold, O LORD, You know it altogether.
5 You have hedged me behind and before,
and laid Your hand upon me.
6 Such knowledge is too wonderful for me;
It is high, I cannot attain it.
7 Where can I go from Your Spirit?
Or where can I flee from Your presence?
8 If I ascend into heaven, You are there;
If I make my bed in hell, behold, You are there.
9 If I take the wings of the morning,
And dwell in the uttermost parts of the sea,
10 Even there Your hand shall lead me,
And Your right hand shall hold me.
11 If I say, "Surely the darkness will fall on me,"
Even the night shall be light about me;
12 Indeed, the darkness shall not hide from You,

But the night shines as the day;
The darkness and the light are both alike to You.
13 For You formed inward parts;
You covered me in my mother's womb.
14 I will praise You, for I am fearfully and wonderfully made;
Marvelous are Your works,
And that my soul knows very well.
15 My frame was not hidden from you,
When I was made in secret,
And skillfully wrought in the lowest parts of the earth,
16 Your eyes saw my substance, being yet unformed.
And in Your book they all were written,
The days fashioned for me,
When as yet there were none of them.
17 How precious also are Your thoughts to me, O God!
How great is the sum of them!
18 If I should count them, they would be more in number
than the sand;
When I awake, I am still with you.
19 Oh, that You would slay the wicked, O God!
Depart from me, therefore, you bloodthirsty men!
20 For they speak against You wickedly;
Your enemies take Your name in vain.
21 Do I not hate them, O LORD, who hate You?
And do I not loathe those who rise up against You?
22 I hate them with perfect hatred;
I count them my enemies.
23 Search me, O God, and know my heart;
Try me, and know my anxieties;
24 And see if there is any wicked way in me,
and lead me in the way everlasting.

4. **Apply the Word.** The Word is our weapon against a negative mindset. It will pierce every dark and negative thought that enters the mind. You need to use the Word of God like a blowtorch; let it cut through the negative thoughts that are trying to take over your mind.

"For the word of God is living and active and full of power [making it operative, energizing, and effective]. It is sharper than any two-edged sword, penetrating as far as the division of the soul and spirit [the completeness of a person], and of both joints and marrow [the deepest parts of our nature], exposing and judging the very thoughts and intentions of the heart" (Hebrews 4:12).

5. **Refuse.** Refuse to allow negative thoughts to become the norm in your life. It can happen quickly and become the driving force in your life, but women who are full of the Holy Ghost will resist this trend and will push themselves to think on good things. "Finally, brethren, whatever things are true, whatever things are noble, whatever things are just, whatever things are pure, whatever things are lovely, whatever things are of good report, if there is any virtue and if there is anything praiseworthy—meditate on these things" (Philippians 4:8).

We cannot win the battle in the mind without Christ as the center of our life.

We cannot win the battle in the mind without standing up to it.

We cannot win the battle in the mind that is trying to destroy our sanity by acting as if it will just go away on its own.

We cannot win this battle in the mind by ignoring it, but we must face it head-on in the name of the Lord!

The vigilant woman
protects her mind, and
resists the enemy.

CHAPTER 2

The Praying Woman

When my knees hit the floor and I begin to war in the spirit, I'm reminded that God is much bigger than what is going on around me.

I could probably write an entire book on prayer since I am very passionate about this topic although I must interject that I am not an expert on prayer. However, I was taught by example by my amazing parents. My late father was the pastor of a large church in Stockton, California, with many campuses in the surrounding areas, and my mother is an author, minister, and prayer warrior. The one thing they both were extremely passionate about was prayer. The church was always praying, whether it was daily 5:00 AM prayer or a twenty-four-hour prayer chain created by the entire church. I remember many times as a young girl when Dad and Mom would pile all us kiddos with our blankets into the car, and we would go to 5:00 AM prayer. Of course, I would often nod off while hearing Dad, Mom, and those in attendance crying to God in prayer. Prayer was always the main staple in our home, but when I was younger, I would think, "All they do is pray." If there was trouble in the church, they prayed. If they needed money to pay the bills, they prayed. If something difficult arose in the home, they prayed. They prayed about everything! I didn't fully understand during those girly stages the incredible power of prayer. But I can tell you now without batting an eyelash that I would not be where I am today had my parents not prayed me out of the hellhole where I found myself in my young adult life. In fact, they prayed me and all of my siblings out of several hellholes, and I am grateful for their steadfast faith.

During certain segments of my life, it seemed I attracted the dark side of things and was equally attracted to the dark side. In other words, I didn't have a desire to fit the preacher's-kid mold, nor did I want to be put in a box and have to fall in line and be like all the others. I hated the politics in religion then and still do. I was often called "the black sheep of the family." It used to bother me, but now if I hear someone refer to me thus (which is rare), I just keep moving because I'm focused on my God assignments. Don't allow the opinions of others to damage your faith in God or to cause you to feel insecure about what you're doing for the kingdom of God. I was the middle child, and we middle children are known for taking risks. We even struggle at a young age, trying to find our own place and identity. That was me in a nutshell. I also was extremely independent, so this combination didn't jell too well for me and the life in which I had been placed. But even though I may have run for a while from my calling, I soon realized that God wasn't going to let me go. No matter how far I strayed, He listened to the prayers of a righteous man and woman, Dad and Mom.

I must give special recognition to my mother, who has exampled prayer since I was a little girl. As I said earlier, I grew up in a home where prayer was not absent at all. In fact, it was the driving force in our home. If you came to our home to stay all night and didn't know anything about prayer, spiritual warfare, and intercession, you might wonder what exactly was going on inside our home. Mom held nothing back when it came to praying. You see, it was normal to be asleep and then to awaken at 2:00 AM by her groanings in the spirit and agonizing cries. I remember many nights, snuggled inside my blankets and lying comfortably in my bed, as I opened my eyes and thought, *Mom is up praying again.* A few minutes later I would roll over, pull the covers close to my chin, and fall back asleep. She would often say that she had felt a burden for a missionary in Africa, China, or the Middle East or for someone in the United States, and she had to war in the spirit until she felt a release and a breakthrough.

I also remember when I was a prodigal child, living in Washington, DC. One morning Mom called me around 7:00 o'clock Eastern Standard Time, which was 4:00 AM Pacific Standard Time. She asked, "Stephenie, are you okay?" I did not know that God had shown her I had been under attack through the night and needed intercession. I had been in the clubs and had gotten involved with the wrong guy, putting myself in a precarious situation. I became fearful and ran down the street at 3:00 AM, desperate to find a safe place. In addition, my cell phone had died. I prayed, "Lord, help someone I can trust to answer the door." I then saw a porch light, ran to the little townhouse, and knocked on the door, and an elderly lady answered. I told her I needed to call a driver to pick me up, so while I was arranging that, she made me some hot tea. She was the sweetest little lady who ended up giving me a lecture about being safe and protecting myself. I will never forget that night. She was an angel in disguise, for she had created a safe place for me and gave me advice only grandmas can. She reminded me of my Nanny Haney who would have made me hot tea or hot chocolate but also would have scolded me about the importance of making right decisions. When my mom asked if everything was okay, I tried to downplay it like everything was fine, but she went on to tell me that the Lord had her up all night praying for my protection.

I finally told her I had been in a dangerous situation and had been fearful that something bad might happen. Stories like these were common growing up in my home. You see, when you are plugged in to the Higher Power, Jesus will begin to nudge you. He will lay people and situations on your heart because a praying woman doesn't ask questions but immediately goes into prayer mode and intercedes for the task before her. I am thankful that my mother is a praying woman and has shown me by example how to pray.

Never think that your prayers are not reaching the heart of God. "For the eyes of the LORD are [looking favorably] upon the righteous (the upright), And His ears are attentive to their prayer (eager to answer), But the face of the LORD is against those who practice evil" (1 Peter 3:12). Prayer is like the air we breathe; we can't survive or overcome difficulties without it. We must commune with Jesus everyday.

I remember many times when the church experienced pressing issues or Mother felt the nudging of the Holy Spirit calling her to go on a fast. She would humble herself and do it. She also did a variety of types of fasts for the sake of drawing closer to Jesus. But I remember one time when she said, "It's time to fast and to get my flesh under control." I did not fully understand that statement at the time, but I sure do understand it now. She would still cook dinner for the family even when she was on one of her extended fasts, and she always felt that her fasts were between her and God. She took Matthew 6:16-18 quite seriously. "Moreover, when you fast, do not be like the hypocrites, with a sad countenance. For they disfigure their faces that they may appear to men to be fasting. Assuredly, I say to you, they have their reward. But you, when you fast, anoint your head and wash your face, so that you do not appear to men to be fasting, but to your Father who is in the secret place; and your Father who sees in secret will reward you openly." Mom was a private person when it came to her fasts and prayer, but my siblings and I not only saw it but also felt the powerful divine connection that permeated the house. Looking back, I now see why Mom was such a fireball and a force to be reckoned with, for she was completely sold out to the cause of Jesus Christ. I am grateful that I grew up where prayer and fasting were considered the main thing. This has helped me to put things into perspective in our current climate. It's helped me to recognize that some things truly do require prayer and fasting like Matthew 17:21 says, "However, this kind does not go out but by prayer and fasting." It's made me more aware that indeed there is only One who is more powerful than anything and anyone on this earth, Jesus!

As a young teenager, I saw God do miraculous things, including healings that caused doctors to shake their heads and declare them miracles. Mom was one of those women who spoke life and faith and who prayed for the miraculous regardless of what she faced. As I got a little older, I remember Mom's holding ladies' prayer, and it was normal to see Acts 4:31 in action there. "And when they had prayed, the place where they were assembled together was shaken; and they were all filled with the Holy Spirit, and they spoke the word of God with boldness." Things began to change in the atmosphere when the women prayed. They would lay hands on the people who had come for prayer, and sure enough, cancers disappeared, growths vanished, sickness was healed, marriages were salvaged, and people were delivered from demonic spirits. Whatever the request was, the women prayed, and supernatural things happened in their midst.

When people pray, miracles begin to happen.

A man in the church in Stockton had black spots all over his lungs, and he and Mom, along with another man in the church, fasted three days and prayed fervently for a miracle. It was a time of spiritual warfare because the enemy did not want this miracle to happen, so he began to attack my mother and the two men. But they kept plugging into praying, fasting, and speaking life. They prayed that the spots on his lungs would disappear, for the doctors were saying that it looked like cancer. After they completed the three days of prayer and fasting, the man with the dark spots on his lungs went back to the doctor in the Bay area for more tests. The doctor was shocked because the spots on the original X-ray had completely evaporated.

Another miracle took place when two daughters brought their mother, who had cancer, into the ladies' prayer. My mother recounts the event.

I have seen God do many miracles in my lifetime! What a great God we serve! I'll never forget the day two daughters brought their elderly mother to ladies' prayer and said the doctors had given her up to die; she had four days to live! They had their hands under her arms, dragging her as she shuffled her feet and tried to walk. They said they had heard about all the miracles God was doing in CLC Ladies' Prayer and asked if we'd pray for their mother. She had stage-four cancer, was very weak, couldn't eat nor walk, had to sip through a straw, had lost her hair, and had a white kerchief covering her head.
*We anointed her with oil and began to pray. I spoke to the cancer to go in Jesus' name! And all the ladies began to take authority, commanding the cancer to be removed, as instructed in Mark 11:22-23 (KJV): "Jesus answering saith unto them, Have faith in God. For verily I say unto you, That whosoever shall **say** unto this*

mountain, Be thou removed, and be thou cast into the sea; and shall not doubt in his heart, but shall believe that those things which he **saith** shall come to pass; he shall have whatsoever he **saith**" (my emphases). As we exalted the Lord, suddenly we felt the powerful glory of the Lord settle upon us! And we all began to praise and worship God. We knew something supernatural had happened. The Holy Ghost was so strong upon all of us, and we felt His glory linger! That was on Wednesday. That afternoon one of the daughters called me and said, "Sister Haney, when we got home, we checked the skin on Mother's body (she had developed a rash from the cancer), and it is totally gone!" Again, we praised God for what He was doing. I'll never forget when I drove into the parking lot by Stockton Christian Academy on Monday morning. I was shocked! There was the little lady with her white kerchief on her head, the one we had prayed for on Wednesday, who could not walk nor eat and who was near death, and she was walking around the parking area without any help from anyone. She held a can of nuts, popping nuts in her mouth and eating them! New strength was in her body; she was like a totally different lady! She had the biggest smile on her face while talking to everyone. It was a powerful, instant miracle God did for a group of ladies who gave themselves to prayer and fasting, seeking the face of God. God gave this sweet lady twenty more years, and she continued giving God the glory until it was time for her to go to her heavenly home. How thankful we are that He still does exceeding, abundantly above what we can ask or think (Ephesians 3:20). He has all power in heaven and in earth, and nothing is impossible for Him to do!

Build Your Own Prayer Closet

"Be persistent and devoted to prayer, being alert and focused in your prayer life with an attitude of thanksgiving" (Colossians 4:2).

Even though I saw all these incredible things taking place while growing up, I eventually had to build my own relationship with Christ. I had to build my own prayer closet and had to discipline myself to spend time with God. I got to a place where I could no longer lean on Dad and Mom to carry me through the ups and downs in life. I could not depend on Mom always to be the one to pray me out of a bad situation, nor could I always call Dad and expect him to jump into action every time I called. I eventually had to learn how to pray myself through my own trials. I had to build my own prayer closet so that when I found myself in a spiritual battle, I could stand on my own two feet. I had to lean on God to give me wisdom and understanding as I navigated the destruction of strongholds in my life. I had to go to God in prayer when it seemed my world was falling apart. I had to pray, I had to intercede, and I had to fast, but those disciplines didn't come without struggle, growing pains, and trials.

As a young adult I experienced emotional trauma, heartache, and hopelessness. I even went through a few seasons of the squelching fires we find in the Book of Job, and I could not see the light at the end of the tunnel because everything was pitch black around me. I didn't even try to understand Job 23:10, "But He [God] knows the way that I take; When He has tested me, I shall come forth as gold." Honestly, I didn't care if I would come forth as gold or not; I just wanted out! My heart was broken, and sadly, I left God hanging and said, "So long, farewell." I became a prodigal, running for my life and trying to find love and peace in all the wrong places. I was consumed with unforgiveness towards my abuser and others. I became jaded with ministry and religion. I had seen my parents go through some hellish seasons while they were giving everything they had to the kingdom of God. I saw them experience betrayals by those who should have been their close friends, I saw my mom cry, and I saw the look on my dad's face that told me he was hurting. It angered me! "Why would I want to be a part of something so cruel and ruthless?" I would ask myself while running from the call. People often think that ministry is glamorous and are attracted to the glittery photos, messages, and lifestyles. But some in modern-day Christianity are busy editing out their flaws, perfecting their platforms, and making sure that each sermon has a level of eloquence so that they can impress the high and mighty when in reality their lives are far from perfect. Many are just going through the motions and are exhausted trying to keep up with everyone else. A stigma in the religious world says, "You're not successful if you aren't going non-stop and doing conferences, going to seminars, or telling people how to lead well." Of course, there is nothing wrong with doing these things, but the pressure to keep up and to look the part is alive and well! If your calendar is not jam-packed, you must be doing something wrong, or you might be viewed as someone who isn't as productive as the one next to you. I guess if you're hitting the pause button or taking a breather, something must be wrong with you, right? Not at all! We need more to hit the pause button more often so ministers can slip into their prayer closets and allow the Spirit of God to restore them, speak to them, and reset their hearts, minds, and souls.

God's ways are not always glamorous to the human heart.

Some are living depressed, some are dealing with major anxiety, and some have even said, "I don't want to do ministry anymore; it's too hard," "Maybe I'm just not built for this," or, "I can't keep up with everyone else." Let me tell you, "Doing ministry God's way is not glamorous nor is it a rosy garden, but with those beautiful roses will come lots of thorns that prick your heart and bruise your soul." We have to go back to the altar, to that first place where we told Jesus, "I do." We have to resurrect our prayer closets and war rooms and to remember that our relationship with Jesus should take precedence over everything else. It starts with prayer. We must pray because desperate measures require desperate prayers, and we are living in desperate times. Many are feeling exhausted because they are trying to keep up with the religious fads, peer pressure, and other churches, so they feel they can't take the time to hit the pause button. While their emotions are going haywire, they are trying to keep up the pretense that they are in top-notch shape because to hit the pause button would mean that someone else will pass them. I say, "Who cares? Let them pass you!" This type of mentality is killing people spiritually left and right and forcing them to wear façades, to be fake.

You do you, do what God is calling you to do, and don't get side-tracked. If hitting the pause button means that you need to tend to an emotional wound you have neglected, it is well worth hitting the pause button. If you need to take care of some things that have been lying dormant in your life, if you need to focus on your marriage, or if you need to repent for some hidden sins and to work on yourself, hitting the pause button is exactly what you need to do. If hitting the pause button is going to help you to rest your weary body and mind, do it. If we want to be fully effective in our prayer closets and in the work of the kingdom of God, taking time to rest is imperative. Even

Jesus told His disciples to rest in Mark 6:30-31: "Then the apostles gathered to Jesus and told to Him all things, both what they had done and what they had taught. And He said to them, 'Come aside by yourselves to a deserted place and rest a while.' For there were many coming and going, and they did not even have time to eat."

It took some time to build my prayer closet.

I didn't build a prayer closet overnight; it took time for me to get there. In fact, I had been a prodigal and wanted absolutely nothing to do with anything that was attached to religion, yet God wouldn't let me go. I was living in Washington, DC, working and learning all I could about politics but eventually began to feel a stirring in my soul and a longing to run back into the arms of Jesus, my heavenly Father. I finally looked into the mirror and, seeing a shattered soul with a broken heart, knew that, in order for me to heal, I needed a Savior. Therefore, I began to trudge slowly back toward the Cross, where I first said, "I do." There Jesus began to do heart surgery on me. He was able to reach deep into places no human hand could reach. He was able to touch the hardness in my heart and to replace it with tenderness. He brought me back to the Cross, where I had to face my hidden sins hanging in my closet. I know my parents' prayers brought me to that place of surrender, for they continued to pray and fast for their prodigal child and never gave up.

Since then I have found that not everything is a battle worth fighting, but I must choose my battles wisely. Otherwise, I am going to live in a constant state of exhaustion and strife. Prayer has helped me reach this place. The human side of me used to take the bait, but now my spiritual radar pipes in and tells me to walk on by and to save my strength for the bigger battles in life. If you want your spiritual radar to be in tune with the Holy Spirit, prayer is what will keep it fully charged, just like you won't be able to use your iPhone or any other type of cell phone if you don't plug it in and charge it. The same applies to us as women of God. Are you plugging yourself into prayer? If not, you will find your spiritual battery is always low.

You must have thick skin if you want to survive in this world.

I have learned that you must have thick skin if you want to survive in this world, and that includes the religious world. Some of our biggest battles come from within the four walls of religion. The late Oswald Chambers penned a great quote, "Spiritual maturity is going from being thin-skinned and hard-hearted to thick-skinned and soft-hearted." We live in a culture where we are easily offended, and all of us are pretty much guilty at times of knee-jerk reactions to anything and everything that comes our way. But can we exemplify Proverbs 15:1, "A soft answer turns away wrath, But a harsh word stirs up anger"? I would think by now that my skin should be pretty thick from all the things I have experienced, but sometimes it is still very thin and defensive. When attacks come our way and we hurt, our flesh automatically wants to retaliate and to defend the hurt we feel. But if we expect to have thick skin, we will need wisdom in everything we say and do. How does one obtain thick skin?

She prays! I know it sounds like such a cliche, but it really is that simple. Pray, "Father, give me thick skin to be able to handle the insults and hurtful things that are hurled my way, and help me to have a soft heart and a tenderness to be able to hear Your still small voice so that I will have Your wisdom to help me walk through this difficult season." Getting into our prayer closets can help us to obtain the thick skin that we need so that we can impact our world for Jesus. At the same time, we can still have a soft heart toward the brokenhearted and diffuse the troubled tongues that seek to lash out at anything and everybody. We must not allow our thick skin to harden our hearts, nor should we become cold to the desperate soul who needs a warm heart to listen. Prayer will fatten your spiritual man and will put some thick skin on your bones. A woman who has thick (spiritual) skin is really just a woman who has allowed prayer, the Word of God, and God's Spirit to control her emotions. Prayer will never steer you wrong, ever!

The foundation to having thick skin is prayer.
The foundation to pushing past fear is prayer.
The foundation to rising above the chaos in life is prayer.
The foundation to becoming a soft-hearted woman is prayer.

Can I just for a moment keep it real? You can't be a praying woman and at the same speak fear, negativity, division words, hurtful words, and doubt into the atmosphere. You must be a woman of prayer if you expect to live above the fray in this journey called life. Being a praying woman will keep you through these difficult times, calamities, sicknesses, and peril in the world. I encourage you to create a special place to pray. I grew up hearing the phrase, "Get into your prayer closet." But we hear the words, "war room," a bit more now since the movie, *War Room*, came out. Whatever you want to call your place of prayer is fine; just make sure you are intentional about praying daily. You might be asking, "What is a prayer closet?" The simple answer is: "It's a special place where Christians go alone, in privacy, to spend time in prayer with the Lord." "But when you pray, go into your most private room, close the door and pray to your Father who is in secret, and your Father who sees [what is done] in secret will reward you" (Matthew 6:6). For me, it helps to eliminate distractions when I have a specific place where I can pray. I know some who pray in their cars when they commute to work. Others pray in their bathrooms because they can find privacy only there. Others have an office to pray in while others turn an actual closet into a prayer room. You have to do what works for you, so find a place for you to take time to pray. Prayer is our lifeline! It is what will get us from plan A to plan B to plan C and then to heaven. Prayer helps to keep us rooted and convicted of things we shouldn't be doing. Prayer also inspires us to fulfill our purpose and to do what God is calling us to do.

The great thing about prayer is that sometimes you don't even have to say much. You can just sit and let your tears speak for you, and you can let God hear your heart. Psalm 56:8 (paraphrased) tells us, "Tears are prayers, too; they travel to God when we can't speak." Many versions say, "Put my tears into Your bottle." If I'm honest, sometimes I don't want to talk because I am either too exhausted or frustrated or just not in the mood to pray. Yes, sometimes my flesh gets in the way and doesn't want to be disciplined, but that's when I push myself up those stairs, into my office, and into a position to receive what I need from the Lord. Prayer should be the first thing we do when we awake because had it not been for Christ, none of us would have a pulse today. By the grace of God, we are where we are today, so why not give Him the brunch option of the day instead of the crumbs and leftovers? If we are not intentional about it, we will fill our daily calendar with business, education, and ministry meetings, along with things of pleasures, and then sadly, God will get the leftovers. "My voice You shall hear in the morning, O LORD; In the morning I will direct it to You, And I will look up" (Psalm 5:3).

Hannah was a praying woman.

When I think about women who prayed in the Bible, I often think of Hannah. We read her story, an open book from which all of us can learn, in 1 Samuel 1. She was a married woman but was unable to have children, and her barrenness began to affect her emotions and her entire life. To make matters worse, her husband, Elkanah, had another wife, Peninnah, and she would try to provoke Hannah. The woman would embarrass Hannah because she was giving Elkanah all the offspring while Hannah remained childless. I can tell you that this arrangement would not work well for me because I would have a really difficult time living with another woman in my household. In addition, I would really have an issue with her gloating over me. My flesh would struggle staying silent, and I would basically have to live in my prayer closet, begging God to deliver me and to put a guard over my mouth before I did some major damage. I guess I need to say aloud that I am thankful I have a man who is married only to me.

Moving on, Hannah's story is still relevant to our times; it applies to many of our situations. Consider that Hannah had to deal with Peninnah and all her taunting and gloating, and on top of that, she had not been able to have any children. This whole scenario would be enough to cause any of us great distressed. As you read, you see that all these difficult things thrown at Hannah took her to a place of deep depression and agony. In fact, 1 Samuel 1:10 (*New Living* Translation) says, "Hannah was in deep anguish, crying bitterly as she prayed to the LORD." Even though she wept bitter tears, something deep within her refused to give up on having a child. She obviously believed that God would answer even if it wasn't in the timeframe she wanted. She held on even when nothing seemed to be changing in her life, and she continued to pray. While she wanted a son, God was preparing the way for a prophet. He needed someone to fulfill His plan, and Hannah would be the conduit. But what if Hannah had not been praying, and what if she had been leading a life of mediocrity? What if she had been too busy focusing on the frivolous things in life and allowing them to take her from her prayer time with the Lord? What if she had given up? Would there even be a Samuel? The old-timers in church used to say, "You have to pray it through." I heard it all the time when I was a little girl, and sometimes I still hear it today. But what does that actually mean? It means that sometimes you continue to knock on the door like Matthew 7:7 directs, "Ask, and it will be given to you; seek, and you will find; knock, and it will be opened to you." You have to continue to trust God even when your dreams are falling apart. God is going to answer. He may provide what you would love to see happen, or it might be something totally different than what you envision. Jesus sees the end at the beginning, so we must trust the outcome even if it doesn't make sense. I think we all can agree that Jesus doesn't always operate in the realm where we can make sense of His works, but we are to walk by faith even when we cannot see it. Hannah's prayers and persistent knocking were eventually answered. She finally gave birth to a son, Samuel, and he became one of the most powerful prophets known in the Bible.

Get back into the ring!

She (the praying woman) felt a stir in her spirit and a nudge in her heart to pray. She knew she could not afford to walk passively through life anymore, for darkness loomed ahead, starting to mess with her soul. She felt weary and fearful and dreaded going into the ring again, but she felt the Holy Spirit beckoning her to go another round. She stepped into the ring, moved into position, and began to knock on heaven's door. She withstood the fiery darts thrown at her, and she began to feel the Holy Spirit moving on her. All of a sudden, Romans

8:26 began to happen. "Likewise the Spirit also helps in our weaknesses. For we do not know what we should pray for as we ought, but the Spirit Himself makes intercession for us with groanings which cannot be uttered."

Never doubt that your prayers are making a difference. Never doubt that God will have the last say. Never doubt that, in His timing, He will fix it in His own way. Never doubt that He cares about your struggles. Sometimes life is hard and sometimes our prayers seem to be hitting a brick wall, but trust God anyhow. He sees what we don't see, and He knows what is best for you and me. Take everything to God in prayer, for he hears the prayers of a righteous man and woman. The last few lines of James 5:16 tell us, "The heartfelt and persistent prayer of a righteous man (believer) can accomplish much [when put into action and made effective by God—it is dynamic and can have tremendous power."

Pray for Discernment

Among the gifts of the Spirit, scarcely is one of greater practical usefulness than the gift of discernment. This gift should be highly valued and frankly sought as being almost indispensable in these critical times. This gift will enable us to distinguish the chaff from the wheat and to divide the manifestations of the flesh from the operations of the Spirit.

– A. W. Tower

We are living in a culture where many are being deceived and led astray. We must discern the situation and the messenger. Don't follow blindly. If you feel a gut check, don't ignore it! We must pray about everything that comes into our lives because we are not fighting flesh and blood but are in spiritual warfare as Ephesians 6 explains.

There are diversities of gifts, but the same Spirit. There are differences of ministries, but the same Lord. And there are diversities of activities, but it is the same God who works all in all. But the manifestation of the Spirit is given to each one for the profit of all: for to one is given the word of wisdom through the Spirit, to another the word of knowledge through the same Spirit, to another faith by the same Spirit, to another gifts of healings by the same Spirit, to another the working of miracles, to another prophecy, to another *discerning* of spirits, to another different kinds of tongues, to another the interpretation of tongues. But one and the same Spirit works all these things, distributing to each one individually as He wills (1 Corinthians 12:4-11, my emphasis).

We can do the following to help us to discern correctly:

1. ***Pray for wisdom, and He will give it to you.*** "If any of you lacks wisdom, let him ask of God, who gives to all liberally and without reproach, and it will be given to him" (James 1:5).

2. ***Test all things. Don't be naive.*** "A prudent man sees evil and hides himself and avoids it, But the naive [who are easily misled] continue on and are punished [by suffering the consequences of sin]" (Proverbs 27:12). It's important to be aware of what is going on around you. This doesn't mean that we are to be suspicious of everyone always, but if we are sincerely praying and seeking God's direction in a situ-

ation, He will reveal the truth. He is not the author of confusion. "For God is not the author of confusion but of peace, as in all the churches of the saints" (1 Corinthians 14:33).

3. ***Know the difference between right and wrong.*** Right is still right, and wrong is still wrong. Do not allow yourself to get caught up in things that look right but that are, in fact, wrong. "But solid food is for the [spiritually] mature, whose senses are trained by practice to distinguish between what is morally good and what is evil" (Hebrews 5:14).

My prayer this past year has been: "Father, protect my husband and me from deception and from things that look right but that are not right. Help us, Lord, to discern correctly so that we can move freely in our calling."

It's time to protect your heart, your mind, your home, your marriage, your relationships, and your calling with prayer.

Don't ignore the red flags in your life; ignoring them won't make them go away. Follow it through, and ask God to help you to stay aware of every ploy and attack from the enemy. When you feel something is off but are unable to determine what it is exactly, seek wise counsel. Safe, godly people will help steer you in the right direction. "Where there is no counsel, the people fall; But in the multitude of counselors there is safety" (Proverbs 11:14). Oftentimes the gut feeling that something is amiss is God's effort to protect you, so don't be quick to dismiss it. If you ignore the red flags in your life, you take the risk of experiencing great heartache, disappointment, and hurt. On one occasion I ignored a red flag that was screaming at me about an unhealthy relationship. Sadly, I justified and made excuses for it. My doing so took me off course, pushed me out of the lane where I had been operating, and messed me up for a while. As a consequence, I had to do damage control in my own life and found myself picking up the pieces of a broken heart. A long process ensued in getting me back to a good and healthy place emotionally, but in time I did heal and was able to move on. But if I would have taken the red flag seriously, I could have avoided dealing with a broken heart along with a deceptive tongue.

I cannot stress this enough: Pray about every decision that you make, and do not ignore the red flags thrown at you. We must not be ignorant, nor should we believe everything that is presented to us as a God opportunity because some are not. Just because it glitters and seems like a good thing does not mean an opportunity is good. We must pray for wisdom, clarity, and discernment, and we must not cave in to deception. Pray earnestly, and God will reveal to you what needs to be revealed. He will keep you on the right path and will never lead you astray. "Ask, and it will be given to you; seek, and you will find; knock, and it will be opened to you. For everyone who asks receives, and he who seeks finds, and to him who knocks it will be opened" (Matthew 7:7-8).

Spiritual Warfare

Impossible battles require prayer-closet time. You are no match against the enemy without God.

These words should be written in the journal of every praying woman about spiritual warfare: "I can't keep it sweet or delicate, nor can I play nice. I have to put on my she-warrior attire because my life, home, dream, calling, family, emotional and physical health, and ministry depend on it!"

When warfare hits, you must be prepared for whatever the enemy brings to the table. In this era, it's imperative that we are always on alert spiritually. We cannot afford to walk on eggshells, nor should we follow (anything or anyone) blindly because we are in a constant battle, spiritual warfare. We often hear of spiritual warfare in the Christian world today. It's almost a common phrase, yet it is anything but common. Spiritual warfare requires that we all wear our armor and that we pray for spiritual intuition so that we can be in tune with our surroundings more appropriately. It is easy to put all our time and energy into something that is really the enemy's distraction. Therefore, we must be spiritually in tune and aware so that we do not become pawns in the hands of the enemy.

For though we walk in the flesh, we do not war according to the flesh. For the weapons of our warfare are not carnal but mighty in God for pulling down strongholds, casting down arguments and every high thing that exalts itself against the knowledge of God, bringing every thought into captivity to the obedience to Christ (2 Corinthians 10:3-5).

What is spiritual warfare? *It's a battle between invisible, angelic forces that affects you and me. We can't see the cause of the war, but we see the effects of it. As another definition, spiritual warfare is basically the battle between us and the forces of darkness.*

We are in a war! Every Christian woman is in some kind of battle today. There is much spiritual activity going on, and if we are not careful, we will become immune to the effects of the spiritual warfare without even realizing it. Romans 8:5-9 lets us know that we cannot properly discern if we are not full of God's Spirit. A carnal mind cannot perceive spiritual things. The word "carnal" is translated from the Greek word *sarkikos*, which literally means "fleshly." Another way to describe it is: "governed by mere human nature and not by the Spirit of God."

For those who live according to the flesh set their minds on the things of the flesh, but those who live according to the Spirit, the things of the Spirit. For to be carnally minded is death, but to be spiritually minded is life and peace. Because the carnal mind is enmity against God; for it is not subject to the law of God, nor indeed can be. So then, those who are in the flesh cannot please God. But you are not in the flesh but in the Spirit, if indeed the Spirit of God dwells in you. Now if anyone does not have the Spirit of Christ, he is not His (Romans 8:5-9).

Many have become casualties of spiritual warfare. Some suffer with emotional wounds from the battle, and some are discouraged, depressed, and defeated. Others have dealt with fatal blows to their marriages, relationships, and family. The enemy has gone all-out trying to destroy the people of God, but we must never throw up the white flag and surrender. God is still in control, and our prayers are gaining ground even if we cannot see it. Even though things may not look good to you and you're feeling discouraged, remember that God is not finished with you. This is why praying women push through even when they do not see the answer and the change, because they know the power in their prayers. Their prayers stand in the gap for many souls today.

The battle lies in heavenly places.

Let's go to Ephesians 6:10-11. "Finally, my brethren, be strong in the Lord and in the power of His might. Put on the whole armor of God, that you may be able to stand against the wiles of the devil."

We cannot be strong on our own and be successful. We must lean on God to give us strength through each difficult season and battle we experience. We must put on the whole armor of God! You may be asking, "What does 'the wiles of the devil' even mean?" The wiles are the devil's schemes, ploys, and all those things he uses to plague your mind. The more you pray, the more pressure hell will put on you, but keep in mind, through prayer you will become more victorious regardless of what hell sends your way. The enemy does not want you to overcome the dark places you face, nor does he want you ever to become free from the deadly grip he has been trying to use to defeat you.

In Ephesians 6:12, we are reminded that we need to put on our war coat because this walk of life requires that we clothe ourselves in some serious (spiritual) battle gear to fend off the attacks from the enemy. "For we do not wrestle against flesh and blood, but against principalities, against powers, against the rulers of the darkness of this age, against spiritual host of wickedness in the heavenly places." According to this verse, we are not fighting against people. We fight something spiritual. The enemy wants us to respond and to react in our flesh and to lash out with our tongue at others because he knows that will keep us busy and distracted from the real battle! The only way we can shake the spiritual wickedness in high places, the demonic powers, and principalities is by prayer, application of the Word, and the whole armor of God.

A spiritual problem requires a spiritual solution.

Many Christian women are in spiritual battles today, and that condition may cause restlessness, anxiety, and even a heavy heart. Then on top of that, many try to fight a spiritual battle with their own flesh and logic. "Now the works of the flesh are evident, which are: adultery, fornication, uncleanness, lewdness, idolatry, sorcery, hatred, contentions, jealousies, outbursts of wrath, selfish ambitions, dissensions, heresies, envy, murders, drunkenness, revelries, and the like; of which I tell you beforehand, just as I also told you in time past, that those who practice such things will not inherit the kingdom of God" (Galatians 5:19-21). This list is pretty straightforward, so we need to adhere to it and ask Jesus to help us to be godly women who are serious about keeping these things out of our lives. We must get in sync with who God wants us to be so that we will respond to the attacks His way. In order to get in sync with the Holy Spirit, we must first be willing to pray and to discard anything that goes against the character of God, for, you see, a spiritual problem requires a spiritual solution. We cannot fight a spiritual battle with our human intellect; it's not going to work. The challenge requires tapping into the supernatural. *Supernatural* means "a manifestation or event attributed to some force beyond scientific understanding or the laws of nature." There is a spiritual battle going on, ladies, and we must remain vigilant and intuitive to what is going on around us.

The She-Warrior

If we want to be fearless, we must put on the whole armor of God because the enemy is going to do all he can to try to defeat us. He does not want one more Christian woman rising, putting on her fearless attire, and combatting his strategy that is trying to bring damage to each and every one of us. If Satan can tempt Eve and cause her to eat an apple that was not on the to-do list by God, he can come in (in disguise) and tempt every one of us with things that we too could fall for. None of us are exempt from temptation and falling; we are all human. This is why we must discern our surroundings and the voices that speak into our lives. This is why prayer should be high on our list of priorities since prayer is a powerful weapon that we need to be using against Satan and his posse. There's a constant war between what you are supposed to do and what you want to do. Our flesh wants things that are not always good for us. This is why it's imperative to be plugged into prayer and the Word. These two ingredients (prayer and the Word) will help us to fight the good fight of faith until the very end.

Where is the location of the battle? Paul told us it is in heavenly places. "For we do not wrestle against flesh and blood, but against principalities, against powers, against the rulers of the darkness of this age, against spiritual host of wickedness in the heavenly places" (Ephesians 6:12).

Let's do a quick synopsis of Paul's words in Ephesians 6:12. This will give us an understanding of what we are up against so we know exactly how to pray for each situation in our life.

Principalities - are ranking demons. God created authority structures in His kingdom, often called "the divine counsel." Satan learned this when he was an angel in heaven, and now he has created his own ranking system. These demons are grouped and ranked according to their purposes. I would also like to highlight how Jesus has set up His ranking system in heaven. Michael is called "one of the chief princes," "your prince," and "great prince" as stated in Daniel 10:13, 21 and 12:1. He is the only angel clearly called an archangel, shown in Jude 1:9: "Yet Michael the archangel, in contending with the devil, when he disputed about the body of Moses, dared not bring against him a reviling accusation, but said, 'The Lord rebuke you!' "

Gabriel is another high-ranking angel whom God uses. His name means "God is my strength." He clearly has a high position among the angels since his name and Michael's are the only ones mentioned in the Bible. It also seems that he is specifically assigned to deliver messages from God to humans. The first mention of Gabriel is in an appearance to Daniel in Daniel 8:16. Gabriel was sent to show Daniel the meaning of a vision he had received regarding the kings of Media, Persia, and Greece (Daniel 8:15-26). Gabriel appeared to him a second time as mentioned in Daniel 9:21 to deliver a prophecy. We also see that he was sent to Mary in Luke 1:26-38 to tell her that she had found favor with God and would bring forth a son named Jesus.

Powers - ability, control, delegated influence, authority. The devil does have power, but he does not have *all* power. God gives us authority over demons, so we do not need to fear the demonic activity that goes on in the spirit world. When fear does come, you need to respond with some Holy Ghost spunk and say, "Not today, Satan!" We must face the enemy with boldness and confidence. Although we are dealing with powers in high places, we have been given authority to cast out demons, to lay hands on the sick, and to be bold witnesses for the Lord. "And these signs will follow those who believe: In My name they will cast out demons; they will speak in new tongues; they will take up serpents; and if they drink anything deadly, it will by no means hurt them; they will lay hands on the sick, and they will recover" (Mark 16:17-18). The demonic forces want to seduce us to be a part of their deceptions of power and supernatural activities. Witchcraft, horoscopes, and psychic phenomenon can seem innocent at first yet are a dangerous influence causing great harm to anybody who gets involved. You don't need your palm read; you just need to be connected to the Great I Am, the Higher Power, Jesus Christ! King Saul did not hear from God, so he went to a medium (1 Samuel 28). He started dabbling with sorcery and ended up destroying his life. Be careful about being impressed by supernatural things, and make sure it is indeed from Jesus Christ and not from hell. This is why you must make sure your identity is in Christ Jesus and not in a person or a group. When you know who you are, you won't mess around with anything that mirrors any type of satanic movement on this earth.

Rulers of Darkness - rule in areas of darkness absent of light and truth. They thrive in ignorance and deception. The devil knows how to scheme and plot for every generation and age. Every age has its area of darkness, and he is the ruler of those areas of darkness. He is ruling in the areas where there is no light. Darkness means there is an absence of truth. Don't accept Satan's lie as your truth. He will make you think that something is a certain way when in reality it's not like that at all. He is the god of deception. Get the facts, and stop believing the devil's lies about yourself and about others. Jesus is the light of the World so we must depend on Him to shine brightly in the dark places in our lives. This is why it's so important to know the Word, and when the devil comes to you with lies, you can refute him with Scripture. John 8:44 reminds us that the devil is the father of lies.

Spiritual wickedness in heavenly places - describes a spiritual hierarchy of invisible and supernatural beings with power. This is what we are dealing with when we are in spiritual warfare. While dealing with spiritual wickedness in heavenly places, we will be bombarded with demonic plots meant to be harmful. Demonic forces scheme for your demise. Satan wants to get the credit when you give up and stop trying. Then he can say, "I got her to that point." "I destroyed her faith in Jesus." "She was praying in the beginning, but she finally gave up because she got tired of the fight." We must never give Satan credit, for to give him credit is like waving a white flag in surrender. The white flag was widely used in the Middle Ages in Western Europe to indicate an intent to surrender, and we aren't about to raise a white flag in surrender to the kingdom of darkness. Satan will try to destroy your faith in God and to distract you from building a life on prayer because he knows how powerful prayer is.

We must get this through our heads and realize that Satan is not fighting us with flesh and blood, but he is fighting us in the warfare of our minds. Are you stressed? Do you feel you are about to lose your mind? Are you restless, exhausted, unable to concentrate, distracted, and crying all the time, and you don't even know why? Are you sometimes angry and don't know why? The spirit of divorce, the spirit of fear, the spirit of deception, the spirit of apathy, the spirit of confusion, and the spirit of division are everywhere. They are spirits of warfare. If we are going to be praying women, we must know how to fight in the spirit. The enemy wants us to react with our flesh. He knows we will not cause his kingdom any damage if he has us distracted to fight spiritual things with physical weapons. But this kind of strategy isn't going to work. We can fight all day with a bunch of words while operating in the flesh, but if we want to do some major damage and thwart his ploys, we have to address it in the spirit. The only way we are going to shake spiritual wickedness in high places, powers, darkness, and principalities is if we pray, fast, apply the Word, and put on the armor of God. It's important to be aware that you are in a spiritual fight. I hear often, "Life happens" or "That's just life." I've said the same thing, and, yes, sometimes it is. But come on, we cannot afford to fall prey to these cute little sayings and phrases because many times it's not just life but actually the opposite. We are on Satan's hit list, targeted throughout the day and during the night. Satan and all his fallen angels are trying to take you out, so you can either make excuses for it or become radical with your prayer life. Be a she-warrior who does not give up easily!

Armed and ready

I'm not talking about an actual gun and bullets but about being armed and ready in the Spirit. If we want to be armed and ready in the Spirit, we must understand what we are fighting. We must be vigilant and we must be strong in the Lord. We are fighting principalities, powers, rulers of the darkness, and spiritual hosts of wickedness in high places.

"Behold, I give you the authority to trample on serpents and scorpions, and over all the power of the enemy, and nothing shall by any means hurt you" (Luke 10:19). God has given us authority, so we must believe it and walk in this truth.

I am calling on all of us to become she-warriors for the kingdom of God. Let's stand at the door of our homes and protect them with vigilance. Let's rise and protect our hearts and minds from the enemy's game plan. Let's refuse to be passive and to just get by, but let us raise our voices in prayer to Jesus, who is the Author and Finisher of our faith. Let us not grow weary, but let us push through every battle, every difficulty, and season that tries to wear us down. We cannot afford to stand idle or to sit back and give up, but we must continue to fight the good fight of faith. If the enemy comes in like a flood, and knocks you down, get back up! True warriors refuse to give up! True she-warriors aren't afraid to get on their knees and to pray until they feel a release and a calm in their spirits. When a soldier is in battle, he doesn't give up after the first round. No! He continues until he fulfills the mission that his commanding officer has given him. Jesus is our commanding officer, and we must do everything possible to fulfill the assignment He delivered to us.

Put on the Armor of God

As praying women, we must understand the importance of the armor of God, and as I've indicated several times now and will continue throughout this book, we are in a spiritual battle. We may not see it, and we may even forget that it's there sometimes. But when the arrows begin to hit home, we push slumber away and rise with determination. We can't afford to play, but we must get serious about this spiritual warfare.

It's not a game. It's real. It's serious. We must put on the armor of God.

We are all guilty of downplaying something that has not personally affected us, but when it hits our personal space, everything changes. The enemy would love nothing more than to fill our minds with so much discouragement and defeat that we think that the war is lost. But it's time to suit up, to become prepared, and to put on the whole armor of God.

The armor of God is essential for survival.

The armor of God is essential for success.

The armor of God is essential for victory.

There is no if about it; we are going to face spiritual warfare.

It's important for us to lay down the carnal weapons, to obey Paul's advice, and to put on the whole armor of God. "Therefore see that you walk carefully [living life with honor, purpose, and courage; shunning those who tolerate and enable evil], not as the unwise, but as wise [sensible, intelligent, discerning people], making the very most of your time [on earth, recognizing and taking advantage of each opportunity and using it with wisdom and diligence], because the days are [filled with] evil" (Ephesians 5:15-16).

The Whole Armor of God

Paul tells us how to be secure and ready for the battle in Ephesians 6:10-18.

Finally, my brethren, be strong in the Lord and in the power of His might. Put on the whole armor of God, that you may be able to stand against the wiles of the devil. For we do not wrestle against flesh and blood, but against principalities, against powers, against the rulers of the darkness of this age, against spiritual hosts of wickedness in the heavenly places. Therefore take up the whole armor of God, that you may be able to withstand in the evil day, and having done all, to stand. Stand therefore, having girded your waist with truth, having put on the breastplate of righteousness, and having shod your feet with the preparation of the gospel of peace; above all, taking the shield of faith with which you will be able to quench all the fiery darts of the wicked one. And take the helmet of salvation, and the sword of the Spirit, which is the word of God; praying always with all prayer and supplication in the Spirit, being watchful to this end with all perseverance and supplication for all the saints.

The apostle Paul listed the pieces of armor worn by the Roman soldiers of his day. He was in prison while he wrote this, so it just makes sense that the analogy of the Roman soldier was portrayed. I find that it makes it easier for us to get a visual on the exact appearance of the armor of God.

Here is the breakdown of the pieces of armor:

1. **Belt of Truth** - Ephesians 6:14 tells us to stand firm, having girded our loins with truth. You may be asking, "How is the belt of truth a part of my spiritual armor?" Girding one's loins means to prepare and to strengthen oneself for what is to come. This is the first thing you do when you put on the armor of God; you gird your loins and prepare for battle. Nowadays, we don't hear too many people saying, "Gird your loins," so some are unfamiliar with the true meaning of this phrase. It's important to understand so we can know why we are to put on every piece of armor laid out before us. This ancient phrase is also used in other places in the Bible. "She girds herself with strength, And strengthens her arms" (Proverbs 31:17). Girding up your loins biblically refers to the act of rolling up the tunic, the common clothing for men and women at the time, and tucking it under a belt or tying it in a knot. They would do this to get the tunic out of the way so that they would have freedom of movement. Men would typically gird up their loins if they were getting ready to engage in battle. We read about this very thing in 1 Kings 18:46: "Then the hand of the LORD came upon Elijah; and he girded up his loins and ran ahead of Ahab to the entrance of Jezreel." This means we need to surround ourselves with the truth and not allow anything other than the truth to enter our personal spaces.

Truth is the belt that holds our armor together. Truth is a crucial component for every woman who is in this spiritual battle; without it we will not be prepared to stand and fight. If your loins are prepared, you are ready for battle. The Roman soldier had to have his belt_on, or everything would fall apart. This is a very important piece of the armor. When we have our belt secured correctly, it will help eliminate the deadly blows that come from the enemy.

2. **Breastplate of Righteousness** - Ephesians 6:14 tells us to put on the breastplate of righteousness to protect our hearts. In the armor of a Roman soldier, the breastplate served as protection for some of the most important parts of the body. Underneath the breastplate lay the heart, lungs, and other organs necessary for life. The breastplate worn by each Roman soldier was generally made of iron and consisted of overlapping pieces of metal with connecting front and back sections. Rounded pieces also protected the shoulders, and the breastplate usually rested on the soldier's hips so the entire weight was not carried on the shoulders. The overlapping pieces allowed for more flexibility of movement. As we wear Christ's breastplate of righteousness, we will begin to develop a purity of heart that translates into actions. It is specially designed by God to protect our hearts and souls from evil and deception. As our lives become conformed to the image of Christ, our choices become more righteous and will protect us from further temptation and deception.

3. **Footwear, shod with the preparation of the gospel of peace**. What do shoes have to do with the armor of God? It may seem strange to consider shoes to be part of your armor, but can you imagine going to battle shoeless? Paul was intentional about our wearing each piece of armor he listed in Ephesians 6, so we must also be intentional about wearing the whole armor of God.

- Shod means "to bind under one's feet, to be in bonds, to tie, to wind, to knit or be at one with." It also has to do with your walk or how you walk out your life from day to day. What you have on your feet is preparation for the gospel of peace. If your feet aren't ready, you're not ready. The word preparation means "prepared base or a foundation which has already been laid." Preparation in Greek means "readiness, to be ready." You will be ready if you wear the proper shoes.

The question is: What kind of footwear are you wearing? I'm not talking about our wedges, flats, and pointy-toe shoes. I'm actually a wedge, platform, and boot kind of girl, but Paul wrote about something totally different. He advised us to stand firm with our feet fitted with the readiness (being fully prepared) that comes from the gospel of peace. We already know that we are going to be tested and tried, so we need make sure that we have the right footwear. "And how shall they preach unless they are sent? As it is written: 'How beautiful are the feet of those who preach the gospel of peace, Who bring glad tidings of good things!' " (Romans 10:15).

A victorious soldier must be prepared for battle. He must study the enemy's strategy and must also be confident in his own strategy, having his feet firmly planted so that he can hold his ground when the attacks come. A Roman soldier would never go to battle wearing ordinary shoes. A soldier's battle shoes were studded with nails or spikes, like cleats; this helped him to keep his balance while in combat. The Roman soldier's journey took him through rocky and rugged terrain and over slopes and dangerous places. This is why they had to have special shoes to help them win the war. They typically wore what is called "the Caliga," a thick-soled half-boot with leather straps tied around and fastened tightly to each foot. The shoe was heavily studded with metal nails to give stability in all forms of terrain. These spikes would help them stand their ground and stomp on the fallen enemy.

If you don't want to be easily swayed, you must have the right shoes on. Satan is going to do everything that he can to move you from a stable place to a place of chaos. Get your she-warrior cleats on, and let's do this! Stand firm, and defend the faith from the enemy's attacks. "You will keep him in perfect peace, Whose mind is stayed on You, Because he trusts in You" (Isaiah 26:3). When we are ready with the gospel of peace, we must be prepared for the attacks that will come from Satan. "Preach the word! Be ready in season and out of season. Convince, rebuke, exhort, with all longsuffering and teaching" (2 Timothy 4:2). If we want to defend ourselves against the arrows of the enemy, we must have confidence in who we are in Christ Jesus. Stand firm in the truth of God's Word, and don't waver under peer pressure. Continue to show yourself approved unto God as commanded in 2 Timothy 2:15: "Be diligent to present yourself approved to God, a worker who does not need to be ashamed, rightly dividing the word of truth." We should always be prepared as we never know when an opportunity may arise to share the good news of the gospel with someone else. We should be willing to answer the call to go into the world and to share the good news to the hungry, the lost, and the broken, for they are everywhere. Let's put our gospel shoes on. Paul made it sound simple when he wrote this; he was committed till the end. "So, as much as in me is, I am ready to preach the gospel to you who are in Rome also" (Romans 1:15).

4. **The Shield of Faith**, Paul told us to take up the shield of faith in order to extinguish all the flaming arrows of the evil one. Another definition explains that it blocks the blows coming from the enemy. For a Roman soldier, a shield was used as a form of protection. The Roman soldier carried this with him in battle and hid himself from the enemy's flaming arrows. The Bible instructs us to hold to our faith because the enemy is trying to destroy it. "Now faith is the substance

of things hoped for, the evidence of things not seen" (Hebrews 11:1). Faith is key in everything we do. Hebrews 11:6 tells us, "But without faith it is impossible to please Him, for he who comes to God must believe that He is, and that He is a rewarder of those who diligently seek Him." Faith is taking God at His Word and acting on it. The enemy attacks us in ways that try to confuse, frustrate, and discourage us. He is always trying to mess with our faith, but our faith can protect us when we experience fear and anxiety. "Have I not commanded you? Be strong and of good courage; do not be afraid, nor be dismayed, for the LORD your God is with you wherever you go" (Joshua 1:9). Even though the fiery darts may come our way, we can still cling to our faith. Isaiah 54:17 tells us, "No weapon formed against you shall prosper." Take up the shield of faith, and block the blows that try to destroy your faith!

5. **Helmet of Salvation-** I grew up hearing, "You must wear the helmet of salvation." You might be asking, "What does that mean?" When the Bible talks about the helmet of salvation, it speaks of protecting the mind. "Because the carnal mind is enmity [hostile] against God; for it is not subject to the law of God, nor indeed can be" (Romans 8:7).

The helmet of salvation is about your thinking. The Roman soldier never entered battle without his helmet. Each soldier puts on his armor and makes sure everything from head to toe is in place. But the last piece of armor donned is the helmet. A helmet is vital for survival, protecting the brain, the command station for the rest of the body. If the head is badly damaged, the rest of the armor would be of little use. In biblical days, this kind of helmet was essential because the Roman soldier's opponent carried a short-handled ax called a battle-ax. When battle-axes were used, heads rolled! If the soldiers did not have helmets, they would get their heads sliced off. The helmet was not just a decorative piece of armor, but it was a defensive weapon designed to save a man's head.

If you do not wear the helmet of salvation as a covering, the enemy is going to wreak havoc in your mind. 1) He will manipulate your emotions. 2) He will make you think that something is wrong with you. 3) He will make you think that you are going to die when you are sick in your body. 4) He will make you think that no one cares about you, and that you are a nobody.

Paul likened our salvation to a helmet, which means that we must know what our salvation includes, inside and out. When our minds are trained and we are thinking correctly, Satan will not be able to play with our thoughts or cause us to go down the wrong path with our thinking. He will have to find someone else to play his mind games with. "We have the mind of Christ" (1 Corinthians 2:16). In order to wear the helmet of salvation, we must be filled with His Spirit. We learn in 1 Corinthians 2:14, "But the natural man does not receive the things of the Spirit of God, for they are foolishness to him; nor can he know them, because they are spiritually discerned."

The helmet of salvation is your safety net.

- You may find yourself in a bad situation, but you will be prepared when you are wearing the helmet of salvation.

- The helmet will defend you from anxious thoughts. Do you struggle with anxiety, unease, or panic attacks?

- Wearing the helmet will protect you from the impact that is meant to destroy you.

- It will help protect you from a hostile world.

- It will help you to keep your thoughts together and to not go negative all the time.

- It will help you with your speech and your outlook on life.

- It will help you with whatever you are struggling with.

Without the helmet of salvation, the enemy has easy access into the mind, will try to manipulate your emotions, and will make you think things that are not true. You may find yourself in a bad spot in life, but you will be prepared to combat his manipulative ploys when you are wearing the helmet of salvation.

6. **Sword of the Spirit** -The sixth piece of armor Paul mentioned in Ephesians 6 is the sword of the Spirit, the Word of God.

"And take the helmet of salvation, and the sword of the Spirit, which is the word of God" (Ephesians 6:17). The sword is both an offensive and a defensive weapon used by soldiers and warriors. In this case, it is a weapon belonging to the Holy Spirit. The Roman soldiers used their swords to protect themselves from harm or to attack the enemy. In both cases it was necessary for a soldier to get rigid training on the proper use of the sword for maximum protection. All Christian soldiers (she-warriors) need the same rigid training to know how to handle the sword of the Spirit properly. Paul did not tell us to take a physical sword to go on a slicing binge. No! the sword of the Spirit means that we pull out the Scriptures and use them as our weapon to combat fear, anxiety, spiritual warfare, sin, and discouragement. "All Scripture is God-breathed [given by divine inspiration] and is profitable for instruction, for conviction [of sin], for correction [of error and restoration to obedience], for training in righteousness [learning to live in conformity to God's will, both publicly and privately—behaving honorably with personal integrity and moral courage]; so that the man of God may be complete and proficient, outfitted and thoroughly equipped for every good work" (2 Timothy 3:16-17).

Since we are in a spiritual battle with the satanic and evil forces of this world, we need to know how to handle the Word properly, Only then will it be an effective defense against evil, and it will also be an offensive weapon we use to demolish strongholds. "For the weapons of our warfare are not carnal but mighty in God for pulling down strongholds, casting down arguments and every high thing that exalts itself against the knowledge of God, bringing every thought into captivity to the obedience of Christ" (2 Corinthians 10:4-5). Hebrews 4:12 tells us that the Word of God is a sword. "For the Word of God is living and active and full of power [making it operative, energizing, and effective]. It is sharper than any two-edged sword, penetrating as far as the division of the soul and spirit [the completeness of a person], and of both joints and marrow [the deepest parts of our nature], exposing and judging the very thoughts and intentions of the heart."

The purpose of the sword of the Spirit (Bible) is to make us strong and able to withstand the evil onslaughts of Satan. Psalm 119:11 (KJV)is a verse I memorized at ten years old, and to this day I quote it on a consistent basis. "Thy Word have I hid in mine heart, that I might not sin against thee."

How do we use the sword of the Spirit? We pull out the Bible, whether it be by memorization, on our phones, iPads, or Kindles, or with the actual book; turn the pages; and begin to speak the holy Scriptures over our minds, our situations, and our homes. Use the sword of the Spirit to speak life into the atmosphere, and start replacing your fleshly desires with the spiritual depth God desires you to reach.

7. **Praying always** - God wants us to be prayer warriors. He wants us to take everything to prayer. "Be anxious for nothing, but in everything by prayer and supplication, with thanksgiving, let your requests be made known to God; and the peace of God, which surpasses all understanding, will guard your hearts and minds through Christ Jesus" (Philippians 4:6-7).

"Pray without ceasing, in everything give thanks; for this is the will of God in Christ Jesus for you" (1 Thessalonians 5:17-18). Praying without ceasing doesn't mean we will be on our knees praying 24/7. So how does one pray continually? With the daily demands on our busy lives, many are doing good if they can kneel in prayer for fifteen to thirty minutes a day. But if you want to spend an hour or more in prayer, you have to discipline yourself since the demands in this culture have made its way into every Christian home. Praying without ceasing means to create a lifestyle of prayer. We can punctuate our moments with intervals of recurring prayer, but we will have to be intentional about doing it. Throughout the day, include God in thanksgiving, praise, requests for direction, and spiritual warfare. Discipline yourself to create an attitude of prayer, and take time to thank God for another day, a vehicle, a job, a bed, food, clean water, and so on. We need to get into the habit of thanking Him for the little things and then glorifying Him for all He's done. We need to get into the habit of covering others in prayer and taking time to intercede when the burden is heavy on our hearts throughout the day. We can incorporate a lifestyle of prayer throughout the day in many different ways, but we need to be intentional about it.

Travailing in the spirit

There are times when we feel a burden, a heaviness to pray more intently, and an urgency, a call to travail. To travail requires an extra amount of exertion. *Travail* is often used in the Bible, along with other words in different translations, such as *anguish, labor pains*, and *toil*. It often refers to the toil and pain a woman experiences in giving birth. "A woman, when she is in labor, has sorrow because her hour has come; but as soon as she has given birth to the child, she no longer remembers the anguish, for joy that a human being has been born into the world" (John 16:21).

Before Jesus went to Calvary, He was in deep travail and anguish as stated in Luke 22:44: "And being in agony [deeply distressed and anguished; almost to the point of death], He prayed more intently; and His sweat became like drops of blood, falling down on the ground."

Even Paul shared his burden in Galatians 4:19-20. "My little children, for whom I am again in [the pains of] labor until Christ is [completely and permanently] formed within you—how I wish that I were with you now and could change my tone, because I am perplexed in regard to you."

You might find yourself stuck in traffic. All of a sudden you get a phone call that is an emergency, but you can pray only in the car. You might be going into a meeting at work and need wisdom; you can pray right then and there before you go into the room. You might be tempted to speak harshly to your co-worker, spouse, or friend, but you can pray a quick prayer even in your mind for God to give you wisdom and to guide your tongue. Listen to the nudging of the Holy Spirit, and make time to find a place to pray alone. If you want victory, be a woman of prayer. Prayer helps us to apply the sword to the correct antagonist. Prayer helps us to stand firm against anything that is not of God. Prayer should be the focal point, for it's the only thing that will get us through the dark seasons of life.

"Now at this time Jesus went off to the mountain to pray, and He spent the whole night in prayer to God" (Luke 6:12).

"Now Jesus was telling the disciples a parable to make the point that at all times they ought to pray and not give up and lose heart" (Luke 18:1).

"Now when Daniel knew that the writing was signed, he went home. And in his upper room, with his windows open toward Jerusalem, he knelt down on his knees three times that day, and prayed and gave thanks before his God, as was his custom since early days" (Daniel 6:10).

"The eyes of the LORD are on the righteous, And His ears are open to their cry" (Psalm 34:15).

"The LORD is near to all who call upon Him, To all who call upon Him in truth" (Psalm 145:18).

"In this manner, therefore, pray:

Our Father in heaven,
Hallowed be Your name,
Your kingdom come.
Your will be done
On earth as it is in heaven.
Give us today our daily bread.
And forgive us our debts,

As we forgive our debtors.
And do not lead us into temptation,
but deliver us from the evil one.

For Yours is the Kingdom and the power and the glory forever. Amen.'" (Matthew 6:9-13).

Never stop praying, never stop believing, and never stop knocking on the door to the heart of Jesus.

As we have just done an intense study on the armor of God, we must also take action with it. It does us no good to talk about it if we are not going to put on the whole armor of God. We must put on each piece of armor and not do it half-heartedly, but we must get some fire in our belly and be full of the Holy Ghost. We must allow God to use us to demolish strongholds and to pierce the darkness in this world.

If we want to be unmovable and unshakable, we need to wrap ourselves in the armor of God.

If we want to be she-warriors for Christ, we must wrap ourselves in the armor of God.

If we want to be victorious, we must wrap ourselves in the armor of God.

As a praying woman,
I call on all she-warriors to put on the armor of God,
move to the front lines,
build your own prayer closet,
and pray.

CHAPTER 3

The Brave Woman

The way you become brave is one terrifying step at a time.

– Bryant McGill

The definition for being brave is: "ready to face and endure danger or pain; showing courage." Throughout history, we see that wars change but the warrior remains the same. We see that methods and even strategies may change, but the warrior still remains the same. We should want to be the kind of warrior who, regardless of what comes her way, will remain bound and determined to stand, be brave, and refuse to cower, run, or hide.

I read a thought-provoking piece by Steven Pressfield in his book, *The Warrior Ethos*. "A messenger returned to Sparta from a battle. The women clustered around.

"To one, the messenger said, 'Mother, I bring sad news: your son was killed facing the enemy.'

"The mother said, 'He is my son.'

"'Your other son is alive and unhurt,' said the messenger. 'He fled from the enemy.'

"The mother said, 'He is not my son.'"

Basically, the mother was saying it is better to face the enemy than to run and hide.

Sometimes you have to stand even when the going gets tough. An older gospel song was first recorded by Donnie McClurkin in 1996, "Stand." It's what I call a timeless song, and it's still sung by artists and worship leaders around the world. When you've done all you can, you just stand. When you've stood your ground and have battled terminal cancer, affliction in your body, divorce, rejection, betrayal, depression, abuse, and disappointment, and when it doesn't seem to be enough and you feel like you're at the end with no relief in sight, what do you do? You stand! Here are the lyrics to the first verse.

What do you do when you've done all you can,
seems like it's never enough;
and what do you say when your friends turn away,
and you're all alone?
What do you give when you've given your all,
and it seems like you can't make it through?
Well, you just stand;
when there's nothing left to do,
you just stand.
Watch the Lord see you through.
After you've done all you can,
you just stand.

I think it's fair to say that many women today are inundated by fear. Fear is roaming freely around us, and doubt has jumped on the bandwagon, too. We are bombarded from all sides with waves of fear and doubt, and even anxious thoughts have increased through the pandemic. It seems like more and more turmoil has been unleashed on this earth, producing much unrest and uncertainty. You need to brace yourself, for when you finally make the decision to stop listening to fear, the enemy will not just go away. When you tell fear where to go and you begin to put your brave shoes on, you better get ready because the adversary is going to pay you a visit. He will do his best to get in your face and to strike fear in you. He is sure to push back on your tenacious spirit so that you will retreat from your game plan, but I encourage you to continue walking bravely through the cobwebs of life. Being brave does not mean that you will never face challenges that tempt you to throw in the towel and to find an easier road. We all struggle with waves of emotions, but you still have the ability to stand up to your fear because Jesus is Your strength. The well-known verse that has been quoted for centuries still rings true. "I can do all things through Christ who strengthens me" (Philippians 4:13). Sometimes you need to give yourself a pep talk and tell yourself that you can do *all* things through Christ because He is your strength.

It may seem impossible for you, but it's never impossible for God. Many of you have heard the powerful story about Moses and the children of Israel. I actually can hear my father speaking on this very topic and can even hear his voice (in my box of memories) loud and clear as he says, "We must not fear, we must step out and be brave, and we must stand and see the salvation of the Lord!" I can see him now with his fist in the air as his passion and burden would take over and he would rally the troops (Christians), challenging them to look fear in the face. He would remind them that God's church is marching forward, that the Lord is fighting for His people, and that we need stay silent sometimes, to remain calm and to trust God with His plan.

Then Moses said to the people, "Do not be afraid! Take your stand [be firm and confident and undismayed] and see the salvation of the LORD which He will accomplish for you today; for those Egyptians whom you have seen today, you will never see again. The LORD will fight for you while you [only need to] keep silent and remain calm (Exodus 14:13-14).

At that moment in this text, the children of Israel stood at the edge of the Red Sea, and right behind them was the Egyptian army. Think about it: this was an impossible situation. In fact, probably most of them had no indication that God was about to do something miraculous that would absolutely blow their minds. Now, keep in mind, the Lord brought this situation into their lives. God had hardened Pharaoh's heart so that he would pursue the fleeing slaves (Exodus 14:4, 8). God had brought them to the edge of the Red Sea while allowing their enemies to be directly behind them. None of this took God by surprise. God wanted Egypt to see that He was Lord so that He, not Pharaoh, would get the glory. " 'I will harden (make stubborn, defiant) Pharaoh's heart, so that he will pursue them; and I will be glorified and honored through Pharaoh and all his army, and the Egyptians shall know [without any doubt] and acknowledge that I am the LORD.' And they did so" (Exodus 14:4). God wanted to teach Israel, who had been relying on Egypt's system and ways, that He was their Deliverer. "Therefore, **say** to the children of Israel, 'I am the LORD, and I will bring you out from under the burdens of the Egyptians, and I will free you from their bondage. I will redeem and rescue you with an outstretched (vigorous, powerful) arm and with great acts of judgment [against Egypt]" (Exodus 6:6). Even though the battle appeared to be between the Egyptians and the Israelites, in reality this was between the Egyptians and the Lord. At times it seems we are surrounded, locked in a horrific situation, and have absolutely no control over the outcome. This is the time to obey the Scripture and to 1) be fearless, 2) stand, 3) see the salvation of the Lord, and 4) stay silent, be calm. The Red Sea was parted, and they walked to the other side. After they were all safe and sound, the Lord allowed the Egyptians to go down the same path as His people did, but once they were in the middle of the sea, He brought the waters back together. Not one Egyptian survived. The Lord showed up and took care of His people. When you don't feel brave and are fearful of what stands before you, remind yourself that Jesus is in control and will make a way even when it seems there is no way. God always has a plan.

We all need strong, female role models in our life.

I encourage you to find someone who is strong in her faith and who has braved the storms of life, someone to whom you can look. It can be a grandmother, a sister, a friend, a mother, or someone you have always admired for her steadfast and unmovable faith. I have several I look to, but the main person whom I look up to is my mother. I grew up in a home with an incredibly strong female role model, and I am thankful for that. My mother was the kind of woman who, if she set her mind to do something, would do it even if it took years to get there. If she felt that spark and fire inside of her soul, she was going to make sure she worked hard to accomplish it. She used to tell my siblings and me to remove "can't" from our vocabulary, and if we ever would say we couldn't do something because it was too hard, she would say, "You can do it; don't speak negativity into the atmosphere." We got frustrated during the moment, but after we accomplished what we said we couldn't, we felt relieved.

In my senior year, I struggled in my math class and honestly thought I might not pass. I told my parents that I didn't need a high-school diploma, but they both said, "Yes, you do. You are going to graduate." I was stressed out, but one of the high-school teachers agreed to tutor me. He made every math problem seem simple, and I ended up passing with a good grade, walked down the aisle, and got my diploma. My mother refused to let me give up. She showed me that in order to do anything great in life, I must apply hard work and discipline.

When I was around fifteen years old, she had gone back to college to complete another degree. I can still hear her playing the piano at 6:00 in the morning. She practiced her classical pieces for the upcoming recital and was determined to do excellent on them. Even though my siblings and I wanted to sleep in on the weekend, Mom remained focused on completing her goal, and we had to endure the early morning playing. Mom was and still is brave in her Christian walk and also in her everyday walk.

She was one of those with whom you didn't want to get into a battle, especially ones that pertained to spiritual things. She is a force to be reckoned with. She may be considered one of the older women in many religious circles today, but that has not fazed her. In fact, if anything she's become more adamant about quoting the Scriptures over her life and over others and speaking faith even when the situation looks impossible. She may move a little slower than she used to. Some might even call her fragile, but just the other day, she began to preach to me over the phone. I heard her voice get fired up, and I said to myself, "Mama still has her spunk!" She is still a fireball for the kingdom of God. I can tell you this, she has a whole ship full of battle scars from the spiritual wars she has fought. Her daily routine still includes getting on her knees and praying over her list of requests, standing in the gap for those who are barely hanging on. Her allegiance is to her Lord and Savior, Jesus Christ, and she still can call on the name of Jesus in a loud voice and rebuke the darkness out of her home because she has fought to reach the place where she is today! She knows what it's like to be brave when she feels frightened, she knows what it's like to be strong when she feels weak, and she knows what it's like to be bold when she has not always felt like going on.

If I could describe my mother in just a few sentences, I would call her not just a fearless woman of God but also a brave woman of God. She has shown my siblings and me, along with thousands of others, how to stay the course even when the ground is shifting. When her faith in God has been tested, she never wavered because her faith has always been in something bigger than herself. Even when all hell breaks loose and the attacks of the enemy are in full force, she continues to trudge forward. She just won't give up but pushes through the difficult seasons that try to take her out. I thank God for the role models we all can look to, for they've made it through the difficulties of life. We can do the same.

For Such a Time as This

Queen Esther stood up to her fears.

When I think of brave women in the Bible, I immediately think of Queen Esther, the woman we all know, admire, and look up to. She had courage; she was brave and stood up to her fears.

Let's go into her world for a moment. Imagine that you can smell the lavender as you walk into this beautiful, nature-driven, and scenic view of complete serenity. You see a luxurious spa surrounded by hundreds of young women, preparing for their encounter with the king. There we watch Esther's being pampered and manicured for that special day when she will stand before the king. She was beautified with oil of myrrh along with other spices and ointments. She was dolled up and had her hair done. I imagine her gown as a gorgeous, handcrafted creation covered with sequins. The servants showered her with the exotic spices and perfumes of their day so that the king would be drawn to her fragrance. Each of the women waited in excitement for her presentation to the king, for he was in the process of choosing a wife for himself. After being presented to the king on that final day, Esther had to wait like the others, and likely her nerves were all over the place as she wondered if she would be the chosen one. Finally, after what seemed like an eternity, the announcement was made that, from the many beautiful young women presented to him, Ahasuerus had chosen Esther as the queen.

However, we must not forget that this was not just about a beautiful young lady being chosen to be the queen of Persia, but God put her in this particular position for a specific purpose only she could perform. She would be the link to saving her people from a man forming a plan to destroy the Jews. I must also note here that, though Esther was of Jewish descent, at the beginning of her reign with King Ahasuerus he was unaware that she was, in fact, Jewish. God placed Esther in the palace for such a time as this, to save her people. She would be the conduit to bring this all to light in the presence of the most powerful man in the kingdom, her husband, the king.

When we read about Esther, we see easily some of her positive attributes. Her humility enhanced another apparent characteristic, self-control. As she moved into the palace to fill her role, the test of her faith and identity stood on the horizon. While she glistened with the royal, fine attire and enjoyed the luxury of her position, she would soon find herself torn between her wish to remain silent and her desire to save her people.

In Esther 4, events began to spiral with her people. Esther's eunuchs and female attendants came to tell her about Mordecai, and she found herself in great distress. Esther was Mordecai's uncle's daughter. He had raised her after her parents' death, so she was probably more like a daughter to him. She learned that he was covered in sackcloth and ashes like many of the other Jews in the kingdom of Persia. She then found out the reason for this display. Haman, who had recently been elevated to a seat of honor higher than all the other nobles in the kingdom, was enraged that Mordecai would not kneel or pay honor to him. Therefore, he wanted to get rid of Mordecai along with his people, the Jews.

Esther 3:8-11 explains why Mordecai wore sackcloth and ashes. Haman was the one person causing Mordecai and the other Jews much anguish.

Then Haman said to King Ahasuerus, "There is a certain people scattered [abroad] and dispersed among the peoples in all the provinces of your kingdom; their laws are different from those of all other people, and they do not observe the king's laws. Therefore it is not in the king's interest to [tolerate them and] let them stay here. If it pleases the king, let it be decreed that they be destroyed, and I will give ten thousand talents of silver into the hands of those

who carry out the king's business, to put into the king's royal treas-
uries." Then the king removed his signet ring from his hand [that
is, the special ring which was used to seal his letters], gave it to
Haman, the son of Hammedatha the Agagite, the enemy of the
Jews. The king said to Haman, "The silver is given to you, and the
people also, to do with them as you please."

As we continue to move through the story of Esther, we see that
Mordecai sent a message, asking her to go into the king's presence to
beg for mercy and to plead with him for her people. But Esther was
afraid because she knew it could mean death for her if she approached
the king without being summoned first. As we dive a little further into
Esther 4, we learn that Mordecai said something to her, capturing her
attention, and caused her to spring into action.

So they told Mordecai Esther's words. And Mordecai told
them to answer Esther: "Do not think in your heart that you
will escape in the king's palace any more than all the other
Jews. For if you remain completely silent at this time, relief
and deliverance will arise for the Jews from another place,
but you and your father's family will perish. Yet who knows
whether you have come to the kingdom for such a time as
this?" (Esther 4:12-14).

During this time, Haman, a prideful man, made plans to kill all the
Jews. Perhaps he whistled as he jotted notes on how he would do it,
for he had the king's ear. And the king was honoring all his requests.
Haman then told his wife and all his inner circle of his plans regarding
the Jews. Meanwhile, Esther finally stood up to her fears and sent a
message back to Mordecai, telling him that she and her servants
would fast for three days.

Then Esther sent this reply to Mordecai: "Go and gather to-gether all the Jews of Susa and fast for me. Do not eat or drink for three days, night or day. My maids and I will do the same. And then, though it is against the law, I will go in to see the king. If I must die, I must die" (Esther 4:15-16, *New Living Translation*).

While Haman rode high, a group of people fasted for deliverance. Haman thought that he was going to get rid of the Jewish race once and for all, but God stood ready to execute His own plan. He prepared Esther to step in and to save her people from this great threat. Esther finally chose to step out in faith even though she knew she was taking a risk. As we move toward the end of this powerful, compelling story about a brave young woman, we see several things take place.

- **Her Identity** - Mordecai reminded her of her identity. I can-not stress this enough, especially in the current climate. It's important for you to know who you are in Christ Jesus. Do you know who you are? "But you are a chosen generation, a royal priesthood, a holy nation, His own special people, that you may proclaim the praises of Him who called you out of darkness into His marvelous light" (1 Peter 2:9). Esther seemed to struggle at first with her identity; she was tied to the king of Persia, the jewels, and the luxuries that came with her status. Most people would tie her identity to the nation of Persia, but something inside Esther caused her to pause and to recognize that she was the daughter of the God of Abraham, Isaac, and Jacob. Her allegiance was to Him first.

- **Fasting** - The first thing Esther did, when she decided she could no longer be silent, was to call a fast. She recognized that she needed to take action before she confronted the enemy. She, her servants, and the Jews all fasted. Mordecai, a devout Jew, would have asked God to protect Esther when she approached the king and to give her wisdom in her approach. After three days of fasting, the queen felt a boldness to face the music, to confront whatever might happen, because she knew she had to save her people. "However, this kind does not go out except by prayer and fasting" (Matthew 17:21).

- **Timing is everything** - Esther also waited for the right time to approach the king about her people and Haman. She didn't just run to the king and have a meltdown for all to see, but she carefully planned everything, fasted first, and then addressed the elephant in the room. Pray for wisdom with the decisions you have to make. "To everything there is a season, A time for every purpose under heaven" (Ecclesiastes 3:1).

- **Surround yourself with the right voices** - She allowed the spiritually intuitive voice of Mordecai to speak into her life. Make sure that the voices who speak into your life are aligned with the Word of God. "The way of a fool is right in his own eyes, But he who heeds counsel is wise" (Proverbs 12:15).

- **We all have a God assignment** - God called Esther to fulfill a specific purpose that would save the Jews. God brought each and every one of us into this world for a purpose. We were not meant just to sit here on earth and exist, but we were called to make a difference in this world for the kingdom of God! We cannot be silent and hide our light under a bushel, but we must fast, pray, help others, and step into what God is asking us to do. We must be about His business. "For if you remain completely silent at this time, relief and deliverance will arise for the Jews from another place, but you and your father's house will perish. Yet who knows whether you have come to the kingdom for such a time as this?" (Esther 4:14).

Esther was strong, brave, and fearless.

Nevertheless, her determination did not come without bouts of fear, distress, and concern about her own safety. She did not immediately jump into action, but after assessing the situation and getting clarity from the right voices, she knew that she was indeed born for such a time as this. Her faith was tested, but she continued moving forward. Thus, God used her to save her people from death.

It's inevitable that our faith will be tested. It's easy to tell others to be brave, but when we are going through our own set of hardships, bravery is the last thing on our minds. Usually, not until we have fought the battle and reaped the benefits of persistency do we realize just how brave we really are. I had someone not too long ago express admiration because of my bravery and consistency. But if truth be told, I don't always feel brave. Sometimes I think 1 am about to lose control and may even have a bit of a meltdown. Yep, I sure do because I know what it means to deal with this thing called fear! Yet I will walk out of those waves of emotions, for I am determined to walk through the seasons in the valley of the shadow of death even when it's difficult. Seeing Esther's faith in action when she found her back against the wall helps us to navigate through those feelings of inadequacy also. Sometimes our faith may not be as strong as it should be, but the important thing is to take a step of faith even when our faith is weak.

A fearless woman has been training a long time for the spiritual battles that are brewing. She knows what it's like to experience tumultuous waves of grief, sorrow, and discouragement from the curveballs thrown her way. I too have dealt with a slew of things that should've knocked me down permanently. Several times I thought I might never become free, but I did. I am brave because of the difficult seasons I have gone through. I would not be where I am today had I not experienced them. Being brave sounds good on paper and great in speeches, but when you are dealing with a chaotic situation outside of your control, being brave isn't on your top list of priorities. You are just thinking about how to survive the brunt of the storm that has hit your life, and better yet you just want it to disappear. You're craving peace of mind and praying for a calm to come into your personal space that has been rattled by the chaos.

"Be on guard. Stand firm in the faith. Be courageous. Be strong" (1 Corinthians 16:13, *New Living Translation*). The Scripture says to "stand firm in your faith"; this verse tells you to be confident in following Jesus. Do not allow anything or anyone to come into your space and try to convince you otherwise. We find out just how brave we really are when we are walking through a hellish season that won't loosen its grip. If you feel you have lost your voice, you will find it again. If you have lost your song, you will find it again. If you don't feel brave and courageous, just know that you are not alone, for we all will face our own mountains of fear, discouragement, vulnerability, and frustration. But there does come a time in your life where you have to get sick and tired of living in fear and need to switch your personal slogan from "Fear" to "Bravery"!

Don't Allow Fear to Cripple Your Faith

When fear attacks, we must not allow it to cripple our faith. We are living in unprecedented times it seems. Fear seems to be swallowing the earth, and everyone wonders what is coming next. During the season of the COVID-19 virus, we have experienced wearing a mask while in close proximity with others, practicing social distancing, and using hand sanitizer until our hands are chapped and feel like sandpaper. As if that were not enough, the unknown lurks and exacerbates the fear and anxiety in many lives. Many have been in panic mode, and I get it because we are indeed living in strange times. Hitting the reboot button sounds like a good thing for this world. At times it feels we have been watching a sci-fi movie, yet we cannot cover our eyes and pretend it isn't happening. I have had hundreds of friends and friends of friends who have become infected with the virus, and sadly, some did not make it through but have died. I have cried a bucketful of tears as I have felt the pain and sorrow of those around me, who are struggling with the sudden death of a loved one. I have lost friends with whom I grew up, so the virus has gut-punched me and has also caused me much sorrow. I have felt an overwhelming compassion toward those who are grieving, including strangers I do not know. Romans 12:15 tells us to weep with those who weep. There has been a lot of weeping this past year. I continue to pray and seek God daily for this broken world that is vulnerable and in need of a Savior. I often think of Psalm 30:5, "Weeping may endure for a night, but joy comes in the morning." We must believe that, in spite of all that is going on, joy is still coming, and the only One who can give us real joy is Jesus Christ. I must admit that I have asked myself a few times during all of this, "Do I trust Jesus? I mean, do I really trust in Him?" The one verse I keep quoting over and again is Psalm 20:7:

"Some *trust* in chariots and some in horses, But we will remember *and* trust in the name of the Lord our God." I know it's easier said than done when our hearts are breaking, but we must put our trust in a sovereign God because only He can fix what is going on in our world. We must never forget that whatever the future brings, Jesus has the whole world in His hands.

You won't always feel brave, but if God is calling you to do something, I encourage you to put one foot in front of the other and to trust Him.

We refer to Gideon as brave, courageous, and passionate. Gideon (like we do) struggled with doubt, fear, and insecurity, yet God called him and used him in a powerful way to destroy the enemy. As we dive into the story of Gideon, we see that he transformed from a man of doubt to a man who became brave and full of faith. He did not allow fear to cripple his faith in God. His story starts in Judges 6, where we see that Israel was greatly impoverished because of the Midianites. In verse 12 the angel told him, "The LORD is with you." Gideon responded by saying, "Please my lord, if the Lord is with us, then why has all this happened to us? And where are all His wondrous works which our fathers told us about when they said, 'Did not the Lord bring us up from Egypt?' But now the Lord has abandoned us and put us into the hand of Midian.." In Judges 6 we follow the dialogue between Gideon and the angel for a while, and in verse 15, Gideon told him that his clan was the weakest and he was the least in his family. Let me insert right here that Gideon did not feel brave at all; in fact, he felt insecure. He felt he was the least in his house. Have you ever felt that you were the least in your inner circle, in your family, at the workplace, or in the ministry of which you are a part? Has the enemy tried to make you feel that you don't have what it takes to go all in for Jesus and that you are not qualified enough to do it? Well, I challenge you to get some Holy Ghost spunk in you and to tell the enemy, "I've had about enough with you!" In Judges 6:16, the Lord responded by saying, "I will certainly be with you, and you will strike down the Midianites as [if they were only] one man." Gideon had a lot of questions for the Lord, but I love what the Lord told Gideon in verse 23. "The Lord said to him, "Peace to you, do not be afraid; you shall not die."

Gideon often gets a bad rap from Christians about his lack of faith and his questions to God, along with what seems to be deep-rooted insecurities. While growing up, I heard his story on many different occasions, and to be candid, I actually love the story of Gideon because I relate so much to him, his questions, and his feelings. I have asked God, "God, are You sure You want me to start this ministry? It's kind of different." "God, are You sure You want to use me?" "Am I qualified for this?" "God, I am not one of those eloquent speakers. I don't have all of the proper quotes and frills." "God, I'm scared. Are You with me?" "I need to feel Your presence right now! I need something because my faith is struggling during this season." "God, I thought You were going to heal him, but You didn't. I feel angry right now, I'm heart-broken, and I don't know if I will ever get over this." "Can You please just hold me for a while because I feel like crying?" "God, where are You?" "God, do I have what it takes? "Hello, God, I need a sign now!" These are real-life conversations I have had with God. Can you relate? Do you too have similar conversations with Him? Do you feel free to pour out your heart to Jesus? He wants you to keep it real with Him. He already knows what you're thinking, so you might as well just pull up a chair and pour it all out to Him.

Let's move on and talk a little bit more about Gideon. We see in Judges 6:25 that the Lord told Gideon to tear down Baal's altar. "Then

Gideon took ten men of his servants and did just as the Lord had told him; but because he was too afraid of his father's household (relatives) and the men of the city to do it during daylight, he did it at night. Early the next morning when the men of the city got up, they discovered that the altar of Baal was torn down, and the Asherah which was beside it was cut down, and the second bull was offered on the altar which had been built." (Judges 6:27-28).

I want to highlight something in verse 27. Gideon was afraid of his family and the people in the town; he was worried about what they would think and do. Therefore, he waited until it was dark outside, and then he went and tore down the altar of Baal. Gideon did what the Lord told him to do, but he still struggled with the fear of what his family and friends would think about him. This story is a prime example for us to follow in that we are to continue moving forward even when we feel bouts of fear and insecurity. As we read about Gideon's life, it's very clear that in spite of his doubt, fear, and questions, God still used him mightily. God used Gideon to deliver His people from the clutches of the enemy. He saw something in Gideon that caused Him to push Gideon out of his comfort zone. Is God trying to push you out of your comfort zone? Are you listening? Are you willing to surrender everything even if it means giving up your own plans? Gideon surrendered even though he seemed to struggle getting there at first because of his insecurities, but he continued obeying God. Eventually Gideon became a confident man of God.

Let's revisit Judges 6:12: "And the Angel of the LORD appeared to him, and said to him, 'The LORD is with you, you mighty man of valor!'" What does that even mean? Mighty men of valor have three distinct characteristics: strength, courage, and passion.

The angel of the Lord spoke this into existence even though Gideon in that moment did not feel strong, courageous or passionate, but he eventually got there. Speak it even when you do not feel it!

It's Time to Step Out

Don't stay in the cave too long. Be brave, step out, and reclaim your place in life. In some seasons, it seems as if hiding in a cave is safer than facing the fear and criticism hovering over your life. One might say that at least in there you don't have to deal with criticism and fear, but that is actually not an accurate statement. Girlfriend, they are lurking about, waiting to pounce, so you might as well get used to it. I think we all can agree that criticism is going to come whether you hide in a cave and do nothing or you choose to step out and do your thing for God!

David hid in caves and still dealt with attacks, criticism, fear, anxiety, and depression. We often find him in the Psalms asking God where He is, and then we hear him asking God to come to deliver him. Here is an example.

Psalm 13

How long, O LORD? Will you forget me forever?
How long will you hide your face from me?
2 How long shall I take counsel in my soul,
Having sorrow in my heart daily?
How long will my enemy be exalted over me?
3 Consider and hear me, O LORD my God;
Enlighten my eyes,
Lest I sleep the sleep of death;
4 Lest my enemy say,

> "I have prevailed against him";
> Lest those who trouble me rejoice when I am moved.
> 5 But I have trusted in Your mercy;
> My heart shall rejoice in Your salvation.
> 6 I will sing to the LORD,
> Because he has dealt bountifully with me.

As you can see in reading this one psalm, David struggled with his emotions like we do. Many of the Psalms resonate with us because David displayed his emotions in his writings and then allowed us to come into his personal space. There we hear his prayers. If you notice in verse 5, he said, "But I trust in Your mercy (unfailing love); my heart rejoices in your salvation." Even though he was frustrated and dealing with a wave of chaotic emotions, he continued to trust in God and to believe that God would get him through his painful season.

Let me ask those of you who find yourself hiding in a cave, trying to survive what you are going through: Are you tired of hiding in the cave? Are you tired of wearing a façade and trying to please people? Are you tired of holding on to things that are keeping you in a unhealthy cycle? That in itself will leave you feeling exhausted and frustrated.

Let's discuss the different cave mindsets that we deal with. In order to be a brave woman, you have to address the issues in your life. God is calling all of us, like He called David, to fulfill an assignment for Him, but we cannot fully step into it or be truly impactful in a positive way if we are bogged down by the baggage that sneaks into our hearts and tries to weigh us down.

1. **Cave of discouragement** - Don't allow feelings of discouragement to linger for too long, and do not throw yourself into the arms of the wrong person to console you. The

Word of God reminds us to cast our cares on Him, and He will sustain us. "Cast your burden upon the LORD, And He shall sustain you; He shall never permit the righteous to be moved" (Psalm 55:22). Even David had to encourage and strengthen himself in the Lord as told to us in 1 Samuel 30:6. "Now David was greatly distressed, for the people spoke of stoning him, because the soul of all the people was grieved, every man for his sons and daughters. But David strengthened himself in the Lord his God."

2. **Cave of insecurity** - We must not allow insecurity to make our decisions or cause us to shrink into the background just because we don't feel qualified or eligible to walk in our calling. "For God has not given us a spirit of fear and ti-midity, but of power, love, and self-discipline" (2 Timothy 1:7, *New Living Translation*). God called us to step out and to be brave women of God so that we can impact the world for His kingdom.

3. **Cave of jealousy** - It's important for us to not get caught up in comparing ourselves with others, for comparing yourself with others can turn into envy and jealousy. Once envy and jealousy get inside, they will get in the way of your moving forward since there is no such thing as mild or moderate jealousy. It will consume you and take over your thoughts. "But each one must carefully scrutinize his own work [examining his actions, attitudes, and behavior], and then he can have the personal satisfaction and inner joy of doing something commendable without comparing himself to another. For every person will have to bear [with

patience] his own burden [of faults and shortcomings for which he alone is responsible]" (Galatians 6:4-5). Proverbs also addresses envy. "A sound heart is life to the body, but envy is rottenness to the bones" (Proverbs 14:30). Solomon said, "Jealousy is as cruel as the grave," and it will take you down if you allow it to grow inside your heart.

4. **Cave of unforgiveness** - Offense usually starts out small. A perception of injustice or maltreatment makes its way into the heart, and then you press rewind and listen to it over and over inside your head until it consumes you. When I experienced abuse, I wanted the person to pay for it, and I wanted everyone in my circle to hate as much as I hated. The unforgiveness grew in my heart until there was no room for anything else. I put on a façade, acting like I had moved on, but it was obvious to everyone around me that I had not. Bitter words had become a part of my vocabulary. When I finally confessed, repented, and forgave the other party, I gained freedom and peace. Forgiveness will lift the heavy weight that is on you and will also give you a peace that passes all understanding. "And whenever you stand praying, if you have anything against anyone, forgive him, that your Father in heaven may also forgive you your trespasses" (Mark 11:25).

5. **Cave of Procrastination** - If you have the go-ahead from God, don't put off your destiny while claiming you're just waiting for the right time. Life is too short for "later." "I will hurry, without delay, to obey your commands" (Psalm

119:60, *New Living Translation*). The following quote really caught my attention because my experience can tell you that this is true: "Procrastination makes easy things hard, hard things harder" (Mason Cooley). Just do it! Don't keep putting it off. Time is ticking away, and we can't press rewind. Moving forward is the only option we have.

The cave mindset will suppress your purpose in life if you allow it to, but once you find the brave woman inside you, you will begin to find your voice again. Those prayers that were once barely a whisper will then turn into a roar. Those little sparks inside will turn into passion and spur you to break the chains of the cave mindset that has been consuming you.

When it seems as if everything is coming against you and you just want to hide in the cave, remember Romans 8:31: "What then shall we say to these things? If God is for us, who can be against us?" Now make it personal. "If God is for me, who can be against me?"

Brave for a cause

Brave women are willing to go all in for Jesus Christ even when the water gets rough. Mark 16:15 tells us to go into the whole world to preach the gospel to every creature, and Jesus said in Matthew 9:37 that the harvest is ready but those who are willing to go are few. But before verse 37 we read, "When He saw the crowds, He was moved with compassion and pity for them, because they were dispirited and distressed, like sheep without a shepherd." All we have to do is look around to see the hollow look in people's eyes, their pain, their sorrow, and their hopelessness. Then we will understand what God is saying here. When we are moved with compassion, we will put our brave shoes on and be willing to do whatever He has called us to do.

Are we willing to step outside our comfort zone to share the gospel of Jesus Christ with the brokenhearted, the lost soul, and the one looking for freedom from a life of bondage? In all seriousness, paying a price and jumping in all the way with Christ are not always appealing. Who really wants to be like the disciples in the New Testament and be thrown into prison, persecuted for proclaiming the name of Jesus, and shunned by various elite groups, all because you won't conform to their agenda? When I read about those who gave their lives to do God's will, conviction grips me. Growing up in mainstream religion here in America, I have observed many things. Many seem to value perfection more than they do prayer, many seem to value the building more than they do fasting, and many seem to value a title and position more than a radical lifestyle for the cause of Jesus Christ. I too bear some responsibility because I've been guilty of having this same mindset. But I have found that when I am sincere in my prayers, asking God to shake me out of my self-absorbed mindset, He begins to chip away at my lustful heart and selfish attitude and sets my mind on things above. Being brave sometimes means going against the tide, going against the norm, and becoming completely and totally focused on the cause of Jesus Christ.

Sometimes it's lonely, sometimes it's tough, sometimes it's heartbreaking, and sometimes we wonder what God is up to because not everything is coming together like we thought it would have or should have. When we tell Him, "I do," we need to take Isaiah 43:2 seriously. When we pass through the water, the rivers, and the fire, He will be with us, and no flame will scorch us. This was written to the Jews who were in captivity in Babylon. God promised them that He would be with them during their affliction and persecution and would give them strength to get past it. So when we feel like taking our brave shoes off, we must forge ahead and be willing to fight against pleasure, apathy, and the modern beds of ease. Instead, we will step out to brave the storms of rejection, misunderstanding, and discomfort.

Women who are brave will continue to persevere and to defy the odds in life. When I think about what it means to be brave, I immediately think of a woman with grit, courage, and an incredibly resilient spirit. Brave women face the storm even when it means the conflict will wreck their own plans.

Below are two stories about young women who were willing to help others and, if necessary, die for the cause of Jesus Christ.

The following story was published in the *Sharefaith* magazine.

Kayla Mueller - She was born on August 14, 1988, and died on February 6, 2015.

Kayla went to Jordan as a humanitarian worker from Prescott, Arizona. She didn't expect that her faith would be tried and ultimately strengthened through an ordeal of capture, sexual torture, and ultimately death. Held by an ISIS leader, Abu Bakr al-Baghdadi, she sheltered two other girls from additional harm, and when a chance for escape came, she decided to stay, telling the other two that her American appearance would endanger them. Soon afterwards, she was killed. She wrote in a letter, "I have surrendered myself to our Creator because literally there was no one else. . . . + by God + by your prayers I have felt tenderly cradled in free fall."

Catherine of Alexandria - She was born in 287 and died in 305.

At only eighteen, Catherine was converting hundreds to Christianity. When a persecution of Christians broke out, she tried to use her influence as the daughter of the Alexandrian governor to persuade the emperor. She went to the emperor and accused him of cruel acts. He could not believe her boldness and called for fifty of the best pagan philosophers to debate her over her Christian beliefs. She won, and her finely crafted arguments even converted some of the listeners. She was imprisoned, and two hundred visitors came to see her, including the emperor's wife. All were converted to Christianity. She was condemned to die by the breaking wheel, but when she touched it, the instrument fell to pieces. In frustration, the dictator finally sentenced her to beheading.

These two young women put on their brave shoes and were willing to follow God's plan for their lives even if it meant death. I see bravery mixed with humility and passion for Jesus Christ in these two. Their testimonies have put an overwhelming desire in me to deny myself and to carry my cross with more of a fervency and urgency. I have more hunger after an endless passion for Jesus Christ, for there is coming a day when we will all stand before Him and will give an account for our lives.

For it is written:
"As I live, says the LORD,
Every knee shall bow to Me,
And every tongue shall confess to God."
So then each of us shall give account of himself to God"
(Romans 14:11-12).

The next two stories are about women who were brave enough to step out and to challenge the status quo.

Rosa Parks - It was bigger than her, but she was ready to bridge the gap. On December 1, 1955, Rosa Parks boarded a bus in Montgomery, Alabama. Instead of going to the back of the bus, which was designated for African-Americans, she sat in the front. When the bus started to fill up with white passengers, the bus driver asked Parks to move. She refused.

She didn't even have to kick, scream, or yell, but she just gracefully sat at the front of the bus. That in itself made a statement. To me she was quite the lady, and I am thankful that she helped pave the way to get rid of segregation. On that particular day she changed the history of America forever.

Florence Nightingale (1820-1910), known as "The Lady with the Lamp," was a British nurse, social reformer, and statistician best known as the founder of modern nursing. She was a member of the Church of England and often prayed for God to give her a task that would define her life. During the Crimean War, she trained and organized nurses to care for wounded soldiers and became known as the founder of modern nursing.

Her experiences as a nurse during the Crimean War were foundational in her views about sanitation. She established St. Thomas' Hospital and the Nightingale Training School for Nurses in 1860. Her efforts to reform healthcare greatly influenced the quality of care in the nineteenth and twentieth centuries.

Florence wanted God to give her a task that would make a difference in her world, and He answered her prayer.

The accounts of these four brave women, along with many others, not only inspire me but also convict me as I see the sacrifices each of them made. The common thread in all of this is that their actions were not just about themselves but about something much bigger! These women came from different walks of life, but each of them stood up to their fears in their own way and would not back down. We need to do the same. We need to stand up to the enemy and say, "No more!" We cannot sit back and allow the current climate to hold us captive.

The enemy would love for us to live in a cycle of fear, but we must continue to stand up to his ploys and devices. He is not letting up, so neither should we. As the world grows darker, we must be brave enough to burn brighter and to shout the good news for all to hear. "Once more Jesus addressed the crowd. He said, "I am the Light of the world. He who follows Me will not walk in the darkness, but will have the Light of life" (John 8:12).

Being brave is sometimes a challenge, and feeling brave is sometimes an even bigger challenge. That is why in 2 Corinthians 5:7 we are told, "For we walk by faith, not by sight." We read in Psalm 56 that David was afraid after being seized by the Philistines. He let us know that he was in a bad place in his life, but his trust was in God Almighty. "When I am afraid, I will put my trust and faith in You. In God, whose word I praise; In God I have put my trust; I shall not fear. What can mere man do to me?" (Psalm 56:3-4).

If you're struggling with putting your brave shoes on and stepping out, I encourage you to become a student of the Word. It has literally revolutionized me to become braver in my calling. The Word fires up my soul and motivates me to want to step out and to do whatever God wants me to do. I grew up hearing both my father and mother preaching hundreds of anointed, convicting, and inspiring messages. But even though I grew up around it, there came a point in my life when I had to know the Word for myself. After I surrendered my heart to Jesus in 2008, I found myself having more of a desire to read the Scriptures. For me it had to become more than just a book sitting on the shelf or an app on my phone, but I had to know it for myself. While I've read the Word since I was a young teen, it seems the last few years I've become quite a student of the Word. I hunger to know it and to understand it in its proper context. I am no longer just taking someone else's word for it, but I am studying it in depth, meditating on it, and allowing God to speak into my heart the revelations He wants to give to me. I encourage you to study the Word of God so you can to understand the Scriptures and the context in which they are given. Connect with others who also desire to know the Word of God in a deeper way. Some passages convict me while other verses cause an attitude of thanksgiving to rise in me. Oftentimes, I need some tissues because the Word of God has me in tears as I feel the push to go into a deeper place with God.

If you want to be a brave woman of God, you must know the Word of God! I feel such an urgency that every woman of God must study the Word and know it for herself. You must let it wreck your preconceived ideas! You must let the Word revolutionize your heart, mind, and soul! Let me add that if you have a difficult time memorizing Scripture, don't be too hard on yourself. I too struggle with it. My husband can literally read something once and have it completely memorized and highlighted in his mind thereafter. Well, that is not how I work. I can read it five times in a row and still be scratching my head trying to remember it. Scripture memorization is probably not my biggest strength. Growing up, I had a few teachers who would send notes home to my parents, telling them that I was always daydreaming and writing things that didn't have anything to do with my schoolwork. Maybe that was a clue that there was another writer in the family, who just needed to be channeled properly. I still do similar things, but I am much more disciplined with my routine. Otherwise, I would never get anything accomplished. But I do a few things now that help me and may also help you. 1) I don't beat myself over the head for not being able to memorize everything. 2) I don't overthink it. That just causes more frustration and breeds feelings of insecurity;

it can also cause you and me to feel useless in our endeavors. 3) I stay the course regardless, and daily I read portions of the Word of God. Consistency is everything.

I encourage you to keep reading, keep putting Scriptures in your notes on your iPhone, keep posting Scriptures on social media, keep putting them on your bathroom mirror, refrigerator, or in your prayer closet on one of your vision boards. "In the beginning was the Word, and the Word was with God, and the Word was God" (John 1:1). Everything else will pass away, but the Word of God will never pass away. The Word of God brings life to this lifeless world. The Word of God will help you to become brave enough to step out and to do what God is calling you to do!

You might be wondering what you are called to do. I can tell you that we are not called to just sit, do nothing, and allow fear to hold us captive. We are all called to go into the world and to share the gospel of Jesus Christ. "Go therefore and make disciples of all the nations, baptizing them in the name of the Father and of the Son and of the Holy Spirit, teaching them to observe all things that I have commanded you; and lo, I am with you always, even to the end of the age" (Matthew 28:19-20). God has each and every one of us on an assignment to help fulfill His vision for His kingdom.

Some are called to brave the uncertainty that lies ahead and to do missionary work in countries that are not pro-Jesus. Some are called to stay right where they are and to brave the homegrown storms they face in their communities, churches, and cities. Some are called to focus on their home and their neighborhoods; some are called to work in specific areas in the world so they can be lights to their co-workers and colleagues. Some are on assignments that are temporary and are fully aware that God will be moving them to another place and assignment, so they are always prepared for the next move. Some are on an assignment to teach and lead new Christians to have a better understanding of Jesus. Others cling to their faith, especially in foreign countries where they are being persecuted, but they are brave enough to keep calling on the name of Jesus and to meet with other Christians in secret locations when possible.

Whatever you feel called to do, do it with everything in you! Time is of the essence. Time is not stopping. Don't waste time, for we don't have time to waste. Find your purpose, and don't waste time doing it!

Put your brave shoes on,
step out,
and go to do your God assignment!

CHAPTER 4

The Bold Woman

It is the bold Christian who can sing God's sonnets in the darkness.

– Charles Spurgeon

Did you wake up today and pray, "Help me to be the bold woman of God that You want me to be; pour Your boldness into me"? This is how serious we should take our role as a bold woman of God. I'm all about being bold, but I want to be in sync with the Holy Spirit so that my boldness does not come across as arrogant, hateful, dismissive, or demeaning. Our culture is in desperate need of Christian women who will stand up and influence those around them to want to run to Jesus and to desire to be more like Him because of what they see Him doing in and through us. Bold women of God are the ones who are going to inspire change in this world, so we must lean on our faith as we continue to tread the murky waters of life.

Being bold looks different than when I was younger. When I was younger and had no experience under my belt, I saw boldness as someone who didn't take anything from anybody, perhaps even a bit mouthy like I used to be, and who wasn't afraid to put someone in their place. While I am a woman who refuses to be a doormat, I also recognize that to be bold in my approach doesn't mean I have to get into a screaming match, nor does it mean that I need to go around feeling obligated to put people in their place. No! Being a bold woman of God means that my walking away makes a very bold statement. I am saying, "You are not going to talk to me like that. I am not lowering my bar and succumbing to your anger. I refuse to get into the boxing ring with you. You are not going to control me, nor are you going to continue to manipulate me. I am not your doormat!" You don't have to scream to be called a bold woman of God. Of course, I must interject here just in case anyone might be confused. We should not avoid healthy confrontation. It's important to recognize when you need to confront something that needs to be addressed and when you need to walk away and say nothing. I find that in most cases walking away is the best policy, especially when emotions run high. I used to get into a huff over petty things and wasted time trying to correct someone who got on my nerves or who had hurt me, just so that I could prove a point. How childish is that? Well, I was that child living in an adult body for a while, but the good Lord took me through some valleys to shake me out of my self-righteous, know-it-all attitude. Now, I can say, "You go right on ahead and spew it all out, but I am on a mission. I don't have time to confront everything that comes my way." An African proverb advises, "The lion doesn't turn around when the small dog barks." You see, a lion is bold, but even he knows that he must rein in his boldness and use it only when the time is right. "Behold, I send you out as sheep in the midst of wolves. Therefore be wise as serpents and harmless as doves" (Matthew 10:16). God is calling us to step out and to be bold but wise in our approach.

Being bold is defined as "showing an ability to take risks; confident and courageous. A bold attempt to solve the crisis." The Merriam Webster Dictionary offers: "Fearless before danger, showing or requiring a fearless, daring spirit."

Bold women come from different walks of life and cultures. We all look different. Some of us are short while others are tall; some have a light complexion while others have a darker complexion. We should never lump us all into the same bag because we are all made with our own strengths, weaknesses, talents, and gifts. God made us so, and He desires to use each of us in His own way. Never think that you don't have what it takes to be a bold woman of God. You do have what it takes, regardless of where you come from.

She was bold and beautiful.

Her name was Abigail. We are introduced to her in 1 Samuel 25. I find her to be quite intriguing. She is described as intelligent and beautiful, and then later we see that she had a boldness inside that she would use to save her household. As you read through her story, it's pretty obvious that her marriage was anything but happy. Her husband, Nabal, was quite the character. His name actually means "foolish," and that is exactly how the story portrays him. Nabal was extremely wealthy, arrogant, and a bit full of himself. He lived near the town of Maon in the hill country of Judea and owned thousands of sheep and goats that he pastured near Carmel. Setting that aside, he also had this beautiful and intelligent wife, Abigail. David also played a huge role in this lady's life. He was on a mission to stay clear of King Saul, who was consumed with destroying him. In 1 Samuel 25:4-9, David sent his men to Nabal to ask for sustenance. Normally, a nobleman would have been glad to offer provisions to the brave men of David who had been guarding his herdsmen and flocks. A young man in Nabal's employ also described David's men to Abigail in verse 16, as "a wall to us both by night and day, all the time we were with them keeping the sheep."

Unfortunately, Nabal was not an honest or noble man. His response was one of arrogance and contempt. "Then Nabal answered David's servants and said, 'Who is David, and who is the son of Jesse? There are many servants nowadays, who break away each one from his master. Shall I then take my bread and my water and my meat that I have killed for my shearers, and give it to men when I do not know where they are from?' " (1 Samuel 25:10-11). David's men returned to him and reported what Nabal had said. David then told his men to put on their swords; they were going to address this man. About four hundred of his men took off with him toward Nabal's house.

So now here comes Abigail. In verse 18 we see that she went into action. She gathered two hundred loaves of bread, two jugs of wine, five sheep already prepared [for roasting], five measures of roasted grain, a hundred clusters of raisins, and two hundred cakes of figs and loaded them on donkeys.

Then in verse 19 she told the servants to go ahead; she was coming behind them. She did not tell her husband, Nabal, what she was doing, but she took the initiative and just did it. "When Abigail saw David, she hurried and dismounted from the donkey, and kneeled face downward before David and bowed down to the ground [in respect]. Kneeling at his feet she said, 'My lord, let the blame and guilt be on me alone. And please let your maidservant speak to you, and listen to the words of your maidservant. Please do not let my lord pay attention to this worthless man, Nabal, for as his name is, so is he. Nabal (fool) is his name and foolishness (stupidity) is with him; but I your maidservant did not see my lord's young men whom you sent" (1 Samuel 25:23-25). Abigail was bold but kind and humble in her approach. By humbling herself and pleading for mercy, she helped save Nabal, herself, their estate, and everyone who worked for them. David eventually calmed down and did no one harm, but God dealt with Nabal after that incident. The proud man died.

What are some of the things we can learn from Abigail?

1. **She stepped out with boldness.** Many women would have run to hide or would not have said anything for fear the repercussions. But Abagail sprang into action and prepared the food and drink for David and his men. She then directed her servants to go ahead. "She said to her young men (servants), 'Go on ahead of me; behold, I am coming after you.' But she did not tell her husband Nabal" (1 Samuel 25:19).

2. **She was humble in her approach.** She didn't come across as controlling, desiring to put David in his place, nor did she scream at him or look like a drama queen. She was gentle and kind and took the high road. Her humble apologies softened the heart of David. "When Abigail saw David, she hurried and dismounted from the donkey, and kneeled face downward before David and bowed down to the ground [in respect]" (1 Samuel 25:23).

3. **She had to do some damage control.** Abigail was desperate to save her home, the employees, and her servants. She could not fix her husband and his ways, but she could show David that she and the rest of her household were not like Nabal and that some good folks lived on the estate. She was able to convey exactly that and found mercy in his eyes. "David said to Abigail, 'Blessed be the LORD, the God of Israel, who sent you to meet me this day. And blessed be your discretion and discernment, and blessed be you, who has kept me from bloodshed this day and from avenging myself by my own hand. Nevertheless, as the

LORD the God of Israel lives, who has prevented me from harming you, if you had not come quickly to meet me, most certainly by the morning light there would not have been left to Nabal so much as one male.' So David accepted what she had brought to him and said to her, 'Go up to your house in peace. See, I have listened to you and have granted your request' " (1 Samuel 25:32-35).

Do They See Jesus in Me?

"Now when they saw the boldness of Peter and John, and perceived that they were uneducated and untrained men, they marveled. And they realized that they had been with Jesus" (Acts 4:13).

Peter and John were disciples of Jesus, and they were questioned by the rulers, elders, and scribes in Jerusalem. Acts 4:13 relates that the authorities were astonished because of the boldness of the disciples, for they perceived them as uneducated and common. Peter and John had walked with Jesus. They had seen Him do many miracles and watched as He reached out to the less fortunate, the broken, the afflicted, and oppressed. But the religious elite (Pharisees) wanted to destroy what Jesus had come to do and wanted to end His message, which the disciples preached. The New Testament for the most part portrays the Pharisees as opponents of Jesus and the early Christians. They were extremely self-righteous and looked down on others who did not act like them. Jesus had no problem addressing them because He discerned their attitudes, spirits, and motives. He spoke to them with boldness in, "Woe to you, [self-righteous] scribes and Pharisees, hypocrites! For you are like whitewashed tombs which look beautiful on the outside, but inside are full of dead men's bones and everything unclean. So you, also, outwardly seem to be just and upright to men, but inwardly you are full of hypocrisy and lawlessness" (Matthew 23:27-28). The real problem was that Jesus was a threat to their religious system, and they could not control Him. Therefore, they began to conspire on how they would snare Jesus and destroy Him. "But the Pharisees went out and plotted against Him, how they might destroy Him" (Matthew 12:14). They wanted to do away with these radical and bold disciples who were turning the world upside down for the name of Jesus Christ. But no one will ever be able to put a lid on this movement that Jesus started.

After the crucifixion, they thought that they had ended Him, but their supposed victory lasted only three days. Through the centuries, many have come to try to silence God's people, but you cannot blow out a fire that is running wild in the hearts of men and women around the world. The church has experienced the Holy Spirit, and no one can blow this thing out! No one can stop it! There will never be a law passed in any country that will tell Jesus what to do. There will never be anyone who can control what God does. He is in control, and He will go wherever He chooses to go! In many third-world countries and places where there is great persecution, the Christians are completely reliant on Jesus because they are not accustomed to having many tangible things to lean on. Jesus is their source and supply! They are bold in their faith because everything that they do is about Jesus.

We must all ask ourselves, "Can they (the world) tell that I have been with Jesus by my speech, my conduct, and my attitude?" Do they see Jesus in me? Am I truly being Christ-like in all that I say and do? Do I give Jesus a bad rap, or am I influencing people to want to know this Christ whom I talk about? Do they desire to know more about Him when they engage with me? Do they see something different in me that causes them to want to change and to become a Christ follower?

Sometimes walking this path is not easy. It takes a lot of discipline, hunger, and intention. It requires us to tame our flesh and to surrender our will to Him. We are being tested all the time with our faith, our attitude, our flesh, our words, our reactions, and so on. But can we still be bold women for God while at the same time continuing to show the love of God.

They spoke the Word of God with boldness.

"And when they had prayed, the place where they were assembled together was shaken; and they were all filled with the Holy Spirit, and they spoke the word of God with boldness" (Acts 4:31).

There it is again; they spoke with boldness. But what did they do before they spoke with boldness? They prayed. If we want to be bold women for God, we must pray first. Otherwise, we will be like everyone else in this chaotic world. Everyone is speaking boldly nowadays it seems, and many are spouting words that cut people off, that bring division, that hurt people, and that wound the hearts of men and women. But I'm talking about being a bold woman of God who can exemplify the love of God through her words even when she is speaking truth. Can we ask Jesus to give us wisdom, grace, and discernment as we move forward and further the kingdom of God? Being bold doesn't seem to be the problem, but can we speak boldly under the influence of the Holy Ghost? After we pray and truly submit our will to His will, we will speak what the Holy Spirit impresses us to say and to do. "Let your speech always be with grace, seasoned with salt, that you may know how you ought to answer each one" (Colossians 4:6).

Set a guard over my mouth, Lord.

The Holy Spirit will convict us if we speak something that goes against the character of God. "Set a guard, O LORD, over my mouth; Keep watch over the door of my lips" (Psalm 141:3).

I pray this often: "Lord, please put a guard over my mouth. Help me to speak what You want me to speak. Father, don't let me get caught up with the lingo (around me) that incites things contrary to Your Word. Help me to keep my eyes on You. Fill me with Your Spirit so that I can have self-control when I feel I'm losing all control. In the name that is above every other name, Jesus!"

Too many folks speak boldly in the flesh, but we need to speak boldly under the influence of the Holy Spirit. In order to be bold women for God, we must be full of His Spirit.

Make sure your boldness is seasoned with love.

Christians should be the boldest people in the world; not cocky and sure of themselves, but sure of Him.

— A. W. Tozer

Being bold doesn't mean being hateful. There, I said it! Some relish the idea: "I like telling it like it is, and if the other person doesn't like it, that's their problem," or, "Well, they are being hateful to me, so I have a right to be hateful back to them." I can't believe I am saying this, but I used to have an attitude just like that. That type of attitude crushes me now and makes me feel heavy-hearted because that is not how a Christian should think or be. The person you are hating may die tomorrow. What if you're the only one standing between him or her and eternity? Your bold words can either speak poison or speak life into that soul. May we all get a burden and a passion for others who are in need of salvation, healing, and peace of mind that come only from Jesus.

The world is watching those of us who call ourselves Christians. They've seen a lot, some are jaded with religion, some have been hurt and wounded, and some want nothing to do with Jesus. When interacting with people in the world, we should make sure we are exemplifying Christ. He was kind to the brokenhearted and to those who were lost and in need of a Savior. Being bold for Jesus Christ does not mix well with being hateful, snide, and dismissive or making someone feel beneath you. This kind of boldness has nothing to do with the Holy Spirit; it's pure flesh. If not careful, we will, without even realizing it, allow ourselves to become influenced by the kingdom of darkness. Satan wants to fill this world with hate and to destroy lives, he wants to bring division and turmoil, and he will use whomever he can seduce to carry out his plan. With this in mind, we need to guard our hearts from the influence of the enemy of our soul. We need more bold women of God to speak up, to proclaim Jesus with love, and to refuse to allow the things in this world to influence us to sling hurtful words at people we should be trying to help. "So then, my beloved brethren, let every man be swift to hear, slow to speak, slow to wrath" (James 1:19).

When speaking truth, we are to speak it in love. "But speaking the truth in love [in all things—both our speech and our lives expressing His truth], let us grow up in all things into Him [following His example] who is the Head—Christ" (Ephesians 4:15). Wounded Christians are barely hanging on, sinners are searching for something real, and some come across as fine but are craving more than they have. Be bold in truth but kind in your tone, for you never know if the one to whom you speak is on the verge of giving up. Your last words could make or break that individual.

Women on a Mission

In John 2, Mary, the mother of Jesus, waited until the right time to push Jesus into His first miracle. She was at a wedding with Jesus and His disciples, and when the wine had run out, Mary told Jesus, "They have no wine." That was the first push, but He responded by telling her His hour had not yet come. He was basically saying, "Mother, it's not time for Me to start doing miracles." For some reason, Mary felt a strong urge to push Jesus, and we see her boldness in John 2:5. She instructed the servants to do whatever Jesus told them to do.

Now there were set there six waterpots of stone, according to the manner of purification of the Jews, containing twenty or thirty gallons apiece. Jesus said to them, "Fill the waterpots with water." And they filled them up to the brim. And He said to them, "Draw some out now, and take it to the master of the feast." And they took it. When the master of the feast had tasted the water that was made wine, and did not know where it came from (but the servants who had drawn the water knew), the master of the feast called the bridegroom. And he said to him, "Every man at the beginning sets out the good wine, and when the guests have well drunk, then the inferior. You have kept the good wine until now!" (John 2:6-10).

Mary knew that it was His time. Her spiritual intuition had kicked in, and her boldness took over as she pushed Jesus to step out and to turn the water into wine.

She was bold, brave, determined, and strong.

In Judges 4, we discover a fascinating narrative. Deborah was one of the judges in Israel and also the only female judge. She was a prophetess and was given the role of a military leader. This lady isn't one of the most discussed women in the Bible, but after reading her story, we can all agree that she was indeed a bold, brave, determined, and strong woman of God. She seemed to have no problem with stepping into uncharted waters and taking risks to further God's agenda, and she wasn't afraid to go into battle. She should inspire us all. She also seemed to dance to the beat of her own drum as she was pretty confident with her role and identity. Judges 4:5 tells us that she sat under a palm tree to do her work (to hear and decide disputes). I would love to sit and to talk over coffee with her, just to learn how the palm tree became a thing for her.

Now Deborah, a prophetess, the wife of Lappidoth, was judging Israel at that time. She used to sit [to hear and decide disputes] under the palm tree of Deborah between Ramah and Bethel in the hill country of Ephraim; and the Israelites came up to her for judgment. Now she sent word and summoned Barak the son of Abinoam from Kedesh-naphtali, and said to him, "Behold, the LORD, the God of Israel, has commanded, 'Go and march to Mount Tabor, and take with you ten thousand men [of war] from the tribes of Naphtali and Zebulun. I will draw out Sisera, the commander of Jabin's army, with his chariots and his infantry to meet you at the river Kishon, and I will hand him over to you.' " Then Barak said to her, "If you will go with me, then I will go; but if you will not go with me, I will not go." She said, "I will certainly go with you; nevertheless, the journey that you are about to take will not be for your honor and glory, because the LORD will sell Sisera into the hand of a woman." Then Deborah got up and went with Barak to Kedesh. And Barak summoned [the fighting men of the tribes of] Zebulun and Naphtali to Kedesh, and ten thousand men went up under his command; Deborah also went up with him (Judges 4:4-10).

As we read this inspiring story, we see that Deborah was ready for the Israelites to face Sisera, the commander of the Canaanite army, and to have a showdown with him. God raised her to speak boldly to Barak and to tell him the plan of action. She directed him to get his marching shoes on because they were going on a mission for the Lord. Barak was the army chief of the Israelites and felt a little reluctant. He wanted her to go with him, so she complied. It seems very clear through the Scriptures that Barak had an enormous amount of respect for Deborah and trusted her so much that he asked her to go with him to face Sisera.

Deborah spoke boldly once again to Barak. "Then Deborah said to Barak, "Up! For this is the day in which the LORD has given Sisera into your hands. Has not the LORD gone out before you?" So Barak went down from Mount Tabor with ten thousand men following him. And the LORD routed Sisera and all his chariots and army with the edge of the sword before Barak, and Sisera alighted from his chariot and fled away on foot" (Judges 4:14-15). The Bible records that Sisera fled from the Israelite army but that Jael, Heber's wife, killed him (Judges 4:21). Although there are just a few verses about Jael, we could say she too was a bold woman. She did not hesitate but instead stepped up to the plate and destroyed the enemy of God's people. On that same day, Deborah and Barak responded to what had just transpired with a song of victory and praise to the Lord God of Israel (Judges 5).

What can we learn from Deborah:

- **She spoke with a boldness** when she told Barak what God wanted him to do. She knew that she had heard from the Lord, and you can hear the urgency as she spoke to Barak with an authority the Lord had given her.

- **She had no fear**. Deborah was the kind of woman who was very matter-of- fact and to the point. This tells us that she was completely reliant on God and took His opinion more seriously than the opinions of others.

- **She obeyed the Lord.** By Deborah's obedience, God used her to bring victory to His people. We hear Christian songs often that say, "I will go where You lead." The question is: "Will you go where He leads even when it's uncomfortable or to places you do not want to go?"

She was a bold woman of God on a mission.

We first hear about our next subject in Acts 18. She and her husband Aquila spent time with the apostle Paul. She was a passionate soul and had a fire deep inside her that pushed her to step out and to boldly proclaim Jesus and His message alongside her husband. After a year and a half of being in Corinth, Paul took Aquila and Priscilla with him to Ephesus. They stayed in Ephesus when Paul left and established a church in their home as written in 1 Corinthians 16:19. "The churches of Asia send you their greetings. Aquila and Prisca, together with the church [that meets] in their house, send you their warm greetings in the Lord." They had a huge impact on Paul and the early church. "Greet Priscilla and Aquila, my fellow workers in Christ Jesus, who risked their own necks for me, to whom not only I give thanks, but also all the churches of the Gentiles" (Romans 16:3-4).

In addition, Priscilla and her husband approached a man named Apollos, to give him a better understanding of baptism. While their approach was perhaps a little bold, it obviously was done with so much grace and kindness that Apollos willingly took their instruction. "Now a certain Jew named Apollos, born at Alexandria, an eloquent man and mighty in the Scriptures, came to Ephesus. This man had been instructed in the way of the Lord; and being fervent in spirit, he spoke and taught accurately the things of the Lord, though he knew only the baptism of John. So he began to speak boldly in the synagogue. When Priscilla and Aquila heard him, they took him aside and explained to him the way of God more accurately" (Acts 18:24-26).

What jumps out at me about Priscilla is how connected she was with her husband. She was bold with the message and stood boldly by her husband, and together they stepped into their calling and ministered to the people around them. They were in it together. In fact, modern Christianity would probably label them as a power couple.

We need more godly and bold women to step up to the plate and to lead the charge.

We are all guilty of having allowed the attitude of the world to get inside our personal spaces and to tell us exactly how a bold woman should act. But the problem is the huge difference between being just a bold woman versus being a bold woman of God. They are not the same, so let's not mesh them. A bold woman of God is focused on the kingdom of God and is more interested with what

God is saying than what the world is saying. "But you will receive power and ability when the Holy Spirit comes upon you; and you will be My witnesses [to tell people about Me] both in Jerusalem and in all Judea, and Samaria, and even to the ends of the earth" (Acts 1:8).

Let the Holy Spirit guide you through these unprecedented times. "And for me, that utterance may be given to me, that I may open my mouth boldly to make known the mystery of the gospel, for which I am an ambassador in chains; that in it I may speak boldly, as I ought to speak" (Ephesians 6:19-20). The Message translates these verses thus: "And don't forget to pray for me. Pray that I'll know what to say and have the courage to say it at the right time, telling the mystery to one and all, the Message that I, jailbird preacher that I am, am responsible for getting out."

Several things we must do if we want to be bold for Jesus Christ:

- A bold woman of God prays.

- A bold woman of God knows the Word of God.

- A bold woman of God knows when to speak up and when to shut up.

- A bold woman of God recognizes that her strength comes completely from God.

- A bold woman of God takes her God assignment seriously.

Repeat after me: "I _____, am a bold woman of God who walks with a confidence that only God can give. I will be bold with my values, my beliefs, and the message of Jesus Christ! No one can take that away from me! I will lean on the Holy Spirit to guide my tongue so that my boldness will be seasoned with love, grace, and mercy. I will lean on the Holy Spirit to guide me to those who are broken, desperate, lonely, and depressed and will speak truth to them with love."

The bold woman,
a woman on a mission,
imparts words seasoned with love, mercy, and grace.

CHAPTER 5

The Focused Woman

Don't let the things of the world distract you.
Focus on your purpose.

— Sunday Adelaja

There I was tucked away in the green, luscious hills overlooking the beautiful ocean in Carmel. It's become the special place I love to visit, an annual event for Asbel and me to enjoy the year's end. As I looked out the big bay window and watched the sunset glisten on the rippling ocean waves, I began to think about the year 2020. I wanted to do something different that would help me to become more focused on the things I had been feeling to do. Some of the projects I had been passionate about had fallen through the cracks and placed on the back burner. I told myself 2020 would be different, but little did I know the trajectory of the upcoming year. Asbel and I were in a good place. We had weathered some pretty excruciating storms and had overcome them, so I was feeling excitement and great anticipation.

After giving it some thought and praying about it, I decided to use "focus" as my word for 2020. I had great plans mapped out and looked forward to a new beginning. I was feeling fresh, motivated, and energized for the new year. But here I am writing this chapter on being focused, and I can honestly say the year 2020, especially from

March onward, indeed had a mind of its own. I think it's fair to say that focusing pretty much on anything has been far from easy for most of us. Yet I continue to tell myself that we will prevail, trudge forward, and keep marching on.

My parents always made New Year's Day a big deal in our home. We ordered takeout from our favorite Chinese restaurant, Mom would usually spread a blanket on the floor, and there we would all sit, enjoying our favorite Chinese dishes. Dad and Mom were big on setting goals, and they would have us write our aspirations and goals for the year. I usually would start by setting a goal to lose some weight because, after all, the pressure to be very thin when I was a teenager was a pretty big deal. I would then move to the more serious things in which I knew I needed discipline.

Now, I find myself here years later, still doing the same thing: setting goals and putting together my to-do lists. Well, 2020 has proven to be quite the roller-coaster ride for us all, and being focused and staying focused has been quite challenging to say the least. It seems every time I set myself to focus on one of my projects, I get distracted. So far, it doesn't seem to be changing pace.

One of the interesting things I have noticed, though, is that some of my goals have changed while going through this difficult time. While America and the world have been in a panic, grasping for answers and in some way looking for a Savior to set them free from this pandemic along with all of the other pressing issues, I have been burying my head in the Word of God and seeking Jesus with everything in me. I would have to say that He has pretty much reset my entire agenda, and I have willingly allowed Him to peel back the layers of my heart. I have found myself daily asking Jesus to help me to get in sync with His plan and His vision. Through this, He has rearranged my aspirations, stretched my vision to fit into His vision, and called me to seek Him more. I have also been purposeful about ensuring that what I have been aspiring to is not just about me but more about fulfilling His plan for my life. I keep hearing the Holy Spirit speak John 3:30 into me. "He must increase, but I must decrease." Yes, I must decrease so that Jesus can increase. We are living in what I call "desperate times." I can hear my parents saying now, "Desperate times call for desperate measures." We cannot afford to be passive or consumed with self, pettiness, and frivolous things, but we must be vigilant, prayerful, brave, bold, and intentional about focusing on what God is trying to do through His people.

Starve your distractions, feed your focus

We are constantly bombarded by distractions, but here's a newsflash. They aren't going away! The pull never ends. You can plan a day to focus on a particular thing you have wanted to do, but I can guarantee you that it won't come without distractions. A popular quote says, "Starve your distractions; feed your focus." It's a great quote but actually doing it is the challenge. We love repeating great quotes about everything and anything, but it takes a lot more work and tenacity to incorporate them into our daily routine. How many times have you written your to-do list, your goals for the week or the month, and a month later you still have some things on that list that have not been taken care of? If you're like me, you get a bit perturbed that you still have some things on your list that should have been handled in a timelier manner. I then ask myself, "Why are they still on my list?" More often than not, I have allowed other things to distract me from completing them.

The big question is: What do we do when we are distracted by things that need to be taken care of immediately? In fact, some things

I wouldn't even necessarily call a distraction but actually more of an urgent item or a serious situation that needs attention immediately! These interruptions need to take precedence over everything else. Sometimes we will be interrupted with things that automatically go to the front of the line, and we have to deal with the new situations without hesitation. Try not to get too frustrated; instead, handle the circumstances, then go back into focus mode, and try again. William Hickson penned an adage in the 1800s, "If at first you don't succeed, try, try, try again." It still rings true.

Maybe you have been distracted by the events in someone else's life or with the news. In fact, the unexpected turn body-slammed you for a bit, and you are just now starting to climb out of the maze of the effects. It's okay! Breathe deeply, get back into the saddle, and focus. If you knew how many situations—and just stuff in general—that have driven into my life and taken me off-focus, you might be scratching your head wondering how in the world this book ever got completed. Well, not to be facetious or anything, but I sometimes wonder that myself. I have to thank God for helping me to focus when it seemed like every distraction in the book was being thrown at me. I have learned that I must be correctly, kind of like mounting a horse. I have to be in the right position if I expect to go at it again. I must mount on the left side of the horse, then I must put my foot into the stirrup, and then I throw myself back into the saddle and get back into focus mode. It's not been an easy ride, but, boy, have I learned some things through the process!

Set Healthy Boundaries

Learn the art of saying no. Don't lie. Don't make excuses, don't over-explain yourself. Just simply decline.

– Unknown

Many feel pressured to say yes to everything and are involved in so many things that they find themselves unable to give quality time to anything. When this happens, no one gets your full attention, and eventually you will feel exhausted. Your focus will become distorted, diluted, and blurred. You can't be everything to everyone, so ask the Lord to help you to make the right choices and to lay on your heart what needs your yes and what demands your no. It is simple to say no when your priorities are in order. In order to focus, you have to say no to something. Finding the balance with these two words (yes and no) is necessary if you want to live a productive life.

Someone might be asking, "What does setting boundaries with distractions have to do with being a fearless woman of God?" Well, my reply would be, "Being focused is perhaps one of the most important things we must do if we expect to be vigilant, prayerful, brave, bold, and rooted." We can't walk the walk and talk the talk if we are allowing distractions to inundate our lives. In order to be a fearless woman of God, we must know how to deal with the distractions that come because they are going to come whether we like it or not. They will push us off course if we allow them to. Many times I have prayed, felt empowered, and stood determined that nothing was going to disrupt my progress, but I found myself smack-dab in the middle of a never-ending list of distractions.

We can be women with lots of fire in our bellies—meaning a powerful sense of ambition or determination—and have it zapped out of us by a simple distraction. We can be excited about what God is doing in and through us, but if we do not rein in the distractions, we will mimic one of those cute little hamsters on a wheel turning round and round but going nowhere. (But we won't feel too cute after going around and around.) Everywhere you look, it seems everyone is busy nowadays, but are they being productive? Ask yourself, "Am I being productive? Am I getting things accomplished, or am I too busy trying to blow out fires that are not mine to blow out?" Just in case you're wondering, you can't fix everything, and maybe you need to hear this reminder, "You're not superwoman!" Sometimes you need to bow out and stop trying to fix everything around you. We can't control other people's behaviors or reactions, but we can control our behaviors and our reactions. We can't do it all but we can do what God has called us to do. If God has called us, He will definitely equip us to execute our God assignments.

How to set healthy boundaries:
1. Communicate your boundary clearly, know where you stand, and then don't retreat on that boundary. Stay consistent. Be firm, honest, and kind.

2. Example of how to respond when someone expects you to step in every time to save him/her from the mess he/she created: "I am unable to continue stepping in for you and fixing it when you are capable of doing it yourself."

3. Another example when someone is pressuring you to do something you are unable to commit to: "I am sorry, but I will have to decline because I am already committed to several other things and need to give them my focus."

4. "But let your statement be, 'Yes, yes' or 'No, no' [a firm yes or no]; anything more than that comes from the evil one" (Matthew 5:37).

5. Self-care, take care of you. We often try to take care of everyone else until we wear ourselves out. Give yourself permission to take some time to renew your mind, body, and spirit so you can give 100 percent to helping others without feeling exhausted and burned out. This doesn't mean that we stop helping people and go into hiding. No, it means that we take the time to rest, to focus on the pressing issues in our own lives, and refocus and refuel when necessary. Hebrews 4:14-16 tells us that that Jesus sympathizes with our weaknesses and that we can approach God's throne of grace with confidence so that we may receive mercy and find grace to help us in our time of need.

6. Don't feel guilty. Some people will try to guilt-trip you for setting a healthy boundary and will also try to manipulate you to remove the boundary. Never allow anyone to make you feel guilty for setting a healthy boundary. Satan wants you to get off track and sucked into a crazy busy lifestyle of overtime work while neglecting your spouse, your family, and other things that should be top priority. It's important to keep things in perspective. "For all that is in the world—the lust of the flesh, the lust of the eyes, and the pride of life—is not of the Father but is of the world" (1 John 2:16).

Staying focused on your to-do list can be quite challenging. We have become accustomed to receiving texts, emails, and notifications within seconds. In fact, if you have your notifications turned on, you are constantly getting pinged every few seconds to remind you, "Hey, I'm here to interrupt you; check me out now!" We can order coffee online and expect it to be ready five minutes before we even pull up for it. We can even order any type of food and have it delivered within thirty minutes or less. We can order things from Amazon and other amazing companies that cater to the needs and wants of people, and frequently we expect it to arrive within twenty-four hours. We are living in a tech-driven culture, and we pretty much have the best of the best at our fingertips. But this consumerism has caused our thoughts to become like a race track because our thoughts are constantly racing, so programming our minds to focus is not for the fainthearted.

- We must discipline our thoughts.

- We must be intentional about it.

- We must (sometimes) reprogram our thinking.

- We must get a plan to combat the unnecessary distractions that come to us all.

I am going to say something that probably won't sit well with everyone, but it needs to be said. If you don't set boundaries with your phone, it will literally take over your life. I noticed a trend in my life not long ago. I really do try to be uplifting on my social media posts and in general with everything I say and do, but I noticed I spent a lot more time on social media and news sites than I really needed to. I found myself scrolling throughout the day, wasting time, and blamed it on the pandemic and chaos of the day. I tried to justify why I was wasting so much time; meanwhile, I would see things that would get me riled up or that would spark fear in me. While many things on social media are encouraging, it also offers a whole lot of mess. Not only secular outlets but also many church folks (Christians) regurgitate toxic, unwholesome, and ungodly conversations, and the ingredients of love, grace, and mercy are overlooked.

I began to feel conviction, and then I had a "come to Jesus" kind of moment. Here's what I heard. "Stephenie, you are wasting so much precious time, which I have given you, on fruitless things. You are getting riled up over things that have no bearing on eternal life. You are reading things that are not uplifting, and you are allowing yourself to get pulled into conversations that I am not a part of. If you want to change the world for Me, you can't do normal, but you have to become radical for Me and allow Me to pour Myself into you." As you can imagine, this convicted me in a huge way and had me crying like a baby. I immediately humbled myself and repented, and honestly, I feel grateful that God cared enough to correct me rather than to let me continue down the slippery slope I was on. I started journaling about it and taking note of how much time I had been spending on the internet versus how much time I was reading the Bible, praying, interceding for people who were in dire situations, reaching out to people in need, and doing a number of other important things that had been neglected. It was not a pretty sight when I finally realized that I was allowing my phone to control me. Yes, this little phone that sits neatly in my soft leather case was controlling my every move, thought, and emotion. "Wow" is right! My perspective began to change. I was not setting healthy boundaries; instead, this tiny little phone with all its texts, emails, news notifications, and everything else that bombards our personal space was leading me like a dog on a leash. I finally had enough. Now I've become one of those people who put the phone on silent when necessary, or I will put it away and sometimes even turn it off. When I'm in my prayer closet, studying the Word, writing, or just taking a break from it all, I am setting a boundary, and I'm not going to feel guilty about it. You shouldn't feel guilty either. It has literally revolutionized me.

I used to be a big people pleaser, so saying "no" hasn't always come easy for me. I guess that comes from being a middle child because I didn't want anyone not to like me or to be upset with me. That has gradually changed since I've come to realize that I will never please everyone at the same time, and I must be okay with that. Why do we think we have to respond immediately to every single text that hits our phone? If you are working on something that requires your full attention, you should not feel obligated to stop every few minutes to answer a text. There will be plenty of time to answer when you take a break or when you are winding down after a long day. I personally believe that social media, technology in general, along with our phones have become our biggest distractions. Before anyone gets too upset with me, just know that I love my phone. It bedazzles me, and it can do pretty much anything I need it to do. The modern-day phone is a great tool for all of us. I use it for social media, notes, daily to-do lists, pictures, videos, texts, emails, and apps. It's not evil, but it becomes a distraction when it controls our lives on a daily basis. Boy, is it controlling a whole lot of people! We want to be fearless women for God, but in order to do that, we must be focused! We must not allow the distractions in life to steal our focus. I have talked to countless people lately, and all of them have told me they have never dealt with as many different distractions as they have through the pandemic. It's a real struggle for many, but hitting the reset and refuel button to get you back on track is possible. You just have to be intentional about doing it.

I'll never forget that first morning when I went upstairs into my office to start writing this book in May 2020. I felt the Lord had laid it on my heart to write. I felt butterflies of excitement in my stomach and was highly motivated to move forward on it because I felt this incredible passion inside. I was ready to go for it. But it's been one thing after another trying to take me away from writing, and I would focus more on the distraction than this book. I found myself saying, "Tomorrow I will for sure start on the book." I repeated this mantra for almost ten weeks before I finally put my foot down and told myself, "Okay, you have to get it together! If it's not urgent, you need to push it to the side. Girl, you better focus!" The constant noise and distractions coming at me like a whirlwind caused me to take extreme measures in setting boundaries.

Remove the Distractions

If you don't take control over it, it will take control over you.
We must be focused on what God is calling us to do.
We must be focused on His plan and His vision for our life.
We must be focused on reaching the world for Jesus.
We must be focused so that we can feel the gentle nudges when He is trying to speak to us. But if we are too busy dealing with the many distractions in life, we will fail to hear the still small voice. "Call to Me, and I will answer you, and show you great and mighty things, which you do not know" (Jeremiah 33:3).

We cannot hear these great and hidden things if we are allowing ourselves to become distracted by the things in this world.

Can you hear the still, small voice?
The Bible gives an example, to which we all should adhere, about listening to the still, small voice. In 1 Kings 18, Elijah called

fire from heaven and showed the people of God that the prophets of Baal were false prophets. "And Elijah said to them, 'Seize the prophets of Baal! Do not let one of them escape!' So they seized them; and Elijah brought them down to the Brook Kishon and executed them there" (1 Kings 18:40). It is important that we do not become distracted by false narratives, false prophets, or for that matter, false anything. After Queen Jezebel heard about Elijah's slaughter of her prophets, she became incensed and threatened to kill him. These prophets of Baal were a part of the ungodly entourage she brought in to manipulate her husband and the people of God. She wasn't going to lie down quietly, but she was going after this great man of God. I encourage you to read the entire story about Jezebel, and you will see that her plan backfired and she eventually was destroyed. But in 1 Kings 19 Elijah found out that Jezebel was threatening to kill him. What did he do? He was, to put it bluntly, scared out of his mind, so he ran for his life and went to Beersheba, dropped his servant off, and kept going until he reached the wilderness. He then prayed that he might die because he was ready to go, but God wasn't through with Elijah. (Let me insert that you might be done, but if God is not done, He will not allow you to lay down and die.) God still had some assignments for Elijah, but Elijah was somewhat depressed. He was tired of the fight. He had become distracted by the voice of the enemy. "He lay down and slept under the juniper tree, and behold, an angel touched him and said to him, 'Get up and eat.' He looked, and by his head there was a bread cake baked on hot coal, and a pitcher of water. So he ate and drank and lay down again. Then the angel of the LORD came again a second time and touched him and said, 'Get up, and eat, for the journey is too long for you [without adequate sustenance].' So he got up and ate and drank, and with the strength of that food he traveled forty days and nights to Horeb (Sinai), the mountain of God" (1 Kings 19:5-8).

An evangelist by the name of Billy Cole was also a prophet. He operated in the gifts of the Spirit, and God used him in a powerful way in America and around the world. He was also used mightily in Ethiopia, where he along with others present would pray for people who had died, and they would watch them open their eyes and live again. He prayed for growths and cancers to leave the body, and they would leave. He rebuked demons out of people, and the people would be set free. He was a radical prophet of God like Elijah. He had been a family friend for a long time, and I had a connection with him and always enjoyed being around him. When I had been living in DC and had begun turning my heart back to God, I drove to West Virginia and stayed a few nights with him and his wife. The stories he told me about these incredible miracles and the unorthodox type of services in the third-world countries held me in utter awe and desire to see them here in America. He also told me that many times he had been ready to go to heaven and that he sometimes struggled with depression. He went on to tell me that, after ministering for hours upon hours in the big crowds, he would stumble into his room exhausted and beg God to take him home because he was ready. But he told me that God told him He still had some more assignments for him to do, and the time for his death had not arrived. During one of the nights of my visit, he prayed over my life and spoke some incredible things into me. In a nutshell, God used him to minister to me, for I had been in a very bad place spiritually and emotionally and was in need of restoration. When I read the account of Elijah, I always think of this precious man of God, Billy Cole, a modern-day prophet and evangelist.

After the fire, came a still small voice.

Mother Teresa said, "Listen in silence because if your heart is full of other things you cannot hear the voice of God."

After Elijah had removed himself from the noise and went to Horeb, the mountain of God, the Lord began to speak to him. "And there he went into a cave, and spent the night in that place; and behold, the word of the LORD came to him, and He said to him, 'What are you doing here, Elijah?' So he said, 'I have been very zealous for the LORD God of hosts; for the children of Israel have forsaken Your covenant, torn down Your altars, and killed Your prophets with the sword. I alone am left; and they seek to take my life' " (1 Kings 19:9-10). Elijah had a "woe is me" attitude. But then the Lord began to show Elijah that He was more powerful than what he had just experienced. "Then He said, 'Go out, and stand on the mountain before the LORD.' And behold, the LORD passed by, and a great and strong wind tore into the mountains and broke the rocks in pieces before the LORD, but the LORD was not in the wind; and after the wind an earthquake, but the LORD was not in the earthquake; and after the earthquake a fire, but the LORD was not in the fire; and after the fire a still small voice" (1 Kings 19:11-12).

Think about that last sentence: "After the fire a still small voice came."

Do you need to find a quiet place where it's just you and God so that you can hear what the still, small voice is trying to say to you? Here are a few questions: Are you addicted to the noise in your life? Are you addicted to busyness? Are you addicted to the distractions so much that you have a hard time sitting still? Are you addicted to doing projects while ignoring your own needs? Has busyness become your identity? Can you hear the nudging of the Holy Spirit calling you to pray, or is the noise too loud in your life? Can you press pause and regroup your thoughts? Can you take five to fifteen minutes and be quiet? There is never going to be a perfect time to still your thoughts and to quiet your heart. You have to take every chance you can get, and train your ear to listen to what the Holy Spirit says. If you need clarity in a situation that has you stumped, try to stop talking and doing, and take time to pray and to listen to the Holy Spirit.

I have a hunger to know God in a more intimate way. I have a passion to become more knowledgeable in the Scriptures. I have a desire to deepen my prayer life. But if I do not discipline myself and my thoughts, I will never reach my full potential in Him. This quote says it best: "Suffer the pain of discipline or suffer the pain of regret." We must push ourselves to become more disciplined and focused even when we don't feel like it; otherwise, we take the risk of putting ourselves into that place called regret.

Just like Elijah, sometimes we have to discipline ourselves to get into a quiet place so that we can hear clearly. The Lord was not in the wind, He was not in the earthquake, and He was not in the fire. After it all calmed down, a still small voice spoke. Elijah was finally in a quiet place where he could hear coherently, without fear and trembling, the still small voice of God.

Beware of the wrong voices.

In order to focus, we must be intentional! In order to focus, we must set boundaries with the wrong voices! The wrong voices can influence you to step into a lane that is not yours. These voices do a lot of damage to women who are sincerely trying to fulfill God's purpose for their lives but are influenced to go at it another way. Many women start out fearless, confident, and determined, but if you are not careful, an opinion from someone can knock you off your feet and cause you to jump into doing someone else's calling or even completely abandon what you were impressed to do. One thing we hear a lot of nowadays is "the Lord told me." Most people mean "I felt the Holy Spirit tell me this, or while reading the Word, I felt impressed to do this and that or to tell you this." This is all great and good, but we need to be careful we do not allow someone with the wrong intentions and motives to manipulate us into giving up our calling and purpose so that we can fit into their personal agenda. I have had some give me a word, and it lined up with the Word of God. I felt that it was on point. I have had others give me a word, and it was completely off the rails and not at all aligned with the Word of God. When I was younger, I was more gullible and would feel special or a part of the "in crowd" when I would receive a word from someone popular. To be quite honest, I was just happy to get a good word. Nowadays, I am more cautious with whom I allow to speak into my life. I am not saying that God cannot use a donkey to give me a word (as He used a donkey to speak to Balaam in Numbers 22), but I can promise, if it indeed is from God, it will be in alignment with the Holy Spirit and with the Word of God. I take everything to prayer now. We should not play games with prophetic voices, for either they are in sync with Jesus Christ or they are not. There is no in between! We cannot afford to believe every voice that comes into our midst just because it sounds good and puffs up our ego. The Bible says to test the spirits. "Beloved, do not believe every spirit, but test the spirits, whether they are of God; because many false prophets have gone out into the world" (1 John 4:1). In a day of so much confusion, fear, and division, we should be vigilant in making sure that the voices speaking into our lives come directly from God and that they are not coming from polluted platforms that are full of self.

David was focused on destroying the enemy.

In 1 Samuel 17, we get an inside look at David, a shepherd boy whom God had anointed to be king over Israel. Of course, we know that even though he was anointed to rule over Israel, that didn't happen for some time. We also know that he had incredible boldness to get into the ring and to fight Goliath, but since he wasn't a trained soldier, some tried to push him aside. But David pushed the envelope a little bit in that he didn't allow the naysayer voices to discourage him. He was determined to get on the field and fight. We could also say that he was kind of naive to how the real world operated, but that didn't stop him either. He insisted on fighting the giant, and even though King Saul tried to discourage him, David would not back down. "Saul said to David, 'You are not able to go against this Philistine to fight with him; for you are a youth, and he a man of war from his youth' " (1 Samuel 17:33). Basically, Saul told David that he was not qualified enough to face Goliath, but David was focused on doing what they all called "impossible." While they were all shaking in their boots and speaking fear into the atmosphere, David had a boldness and was determined to face the giant head-on. He planned on killing Goliath so that Israel could be set free from the constant taunts and terror hovering over them. Yet when he stood before the king, he was told, "You can't do it!" You see, when you have a vision to accomplish something significant, you will always be challenged by some who will tell you why it can't be done and, even more specifically, why you can't do it! But we should all be aware that the person telling David he could not do something great was actually the one living in fear and unwilling to do what needed to be done. King Saul should have been leading the charge, but instead God raised up a nobody and made him somebody. Saul did not even recognize that David was anointed. That is how out of touch Saul was. Even though David had no one cheering him on, he still had the tenacity and stamina to go out to face the giant.

King Saul finally realized that he was not going to convince David to stand down, so he offered him his armor. But David was not comfortable wearing King Saul's armor because he had his armor already on. I have a message, entitled "Wear your own armor." In other words, don't get stuck on trying to wear someone else's armor and forget that you are called to wear your own armor. Stay focused! David was focused. His brothers could not get him off focus, nor could Saul convince him to do it his way. This is a prime example of what it's like to stay focused (when God has you on a mission) even when other voices are trying to discourage you from doing what you know you need to do.

Never allow anyone to talk you out of what you know God has called you to do.

David's brothers tried to talk him out of going into the arena to kill Goliath, and as we know, even Saul tried to persuade David to wear what was expected of him when going into battle. But David removed the armor and did something unorthodox. He chose five smooth stones from a brook and put them in his shepherd's bag. All he had was a sling in his hand and five smooth stones, but he walked in confidence toward Goliath.

He was focused on killing the giant! He was focused on the mission! He was focused on his God assignment! The last voice David had to overcome was the voice of Goliath. As David began walking toward his target, Goliath said: " 'Am I a dog, that you come at me with sticks?' And the Philistine cursed David by his gods. And the Philistine said to David, 'Come to me, and I will give your flesh to the birds of the air and the beasts of the field!' " (1 Samuel 17:43-44). No wonder everyone was scared of this giant! He towered over everyone and threw insults and threats to the people of Israel, but all his boasts were getting ready to come to an end.

The enemy always tries to discourage you with fear.

When the enemy comes into our lives, he will try to attack our faith in God. I would like you to picture this. Saul and the Israelites served the Lord Almighty, who was more powerful than any difficult situation they had to endure, and there was no comparison whatsoever to the false gods the Philistines worshipped. Yet Saul along with the others allowed Goliath's words to penetrate their hearts and allowed fear (that came from the enemy) to overcome them. What Goliath said he was going to do to David would cause most people to tremble in fear and run. No one wants to be killed and then fed to wild animals. Thankfully though, David did not give in to the voice of the enemy, nor did he retreat or and let his guard down. Something in David caused him to stay the course. He was not going to let anything or anyone deter him from this mission. It's quite amazing that not even the giant who spewed these venomous verbal assaults could stop David. The calling in David's heart was much greater than the giant in front of him.

God has a calling on our lives. He has a plan for us as Jeremiah 29:11 tells us: " 'For I know the thoughts that I think toward you, says the Lord, thoughts of peace and not of evil, to give you a future and a hope.' " But if we listen to the voice of the enemy, we will become distracted and will find ourselves vacillating through life. David decided that, in spite of all of the voices coming at him, he would choose to believe in the calling God had placed on his life. He refused to listen to the voices that peddled fear into the ears of the people around him. Once he faced the giant, David went on to accomplish far greater things than he could even imagine. David was focused on one thing, and that was to fulfill God's plan for his life that day. If David can remove the wrong voices, plow through times of uncertainty, and still be completely focused, so can we. Step out in confidence, and focus on the assignment God has called you to do.

I've often heard it said that if the enemy can't destroy you, he will try to distract you. Let's get one thing straight: he is going to use whatever and whomever to try to get you to focus on things that have nothing to do with where God wants to take you. You need to be aware, vigilant, and attentive to the distractions that the enemy throws your way. As a matter of fact, Jesus understands the distractions that come to us all, for, you see, he had to deal with Satan when he was in solitude and on a fast. Matthew 4:1 tells us that the Spirit led Jesus into the wilderness to be tempted by the devil. After forty days and nights of fasting, He was hungry. Of course, the devil made his entrance just then and began to try to entice Jesus to turn stones into bread. Jesus responded with the Word! The chapter goes on to tell us that Satan tried to tempt Jesus several times. But by verse 10 Jesus had enough and said, "Away with you, Satan! For it is written, 'You shall worship the LORD your God, and Him only you shall serve.' " After the devil had left Him, the angels came and ministered to Jesus.

There are times when we need to react like Jesus and say, "Enough, Satan, away with you!" I like the way the *Amplified Version* says it, "Go away, Satan!" When you're focused on the mission, you don't have time to play games, nor do you have time to get into arguments that are going nowhere. You have to end the conversation so that you can focus on the mission.

It's time to handle the distraction.

I have come to realize that telling myself to stay focused on a task and a goal is a lot easier said than done. I have tried it and have failed miserably many times. The first thing you must address is the distraction hanging over your head.

Here are a few things we can do to eliminate the distractions.

- Turn off the notifications on your phone, put the phone on silent, or turn the phone off completely for an hour or even longer if you are able to.

- Make a point daily and as often as you can to find a quiet place, and take some time to meditate on the Word of God. (It can be on a break at work or in your car, office, bathroom, or bedroom, or outside.)

- Rest. Make sure you are getting enough sleep because a lack of sleep makes us feel sluggish and will affect our focus and decisions in life.

- Set realistic goals. Be specific and then set a timeline.

- Pray over what you are trying to accomplish. If you have a deadline, ask Jesus to help you to focus and to flow through you so that you can complete it on time.

- Set boundaries with the wrong influences that are constantly distracting you and causing you to get off track. (Ask the Lord to remove the wrong distractions from your life.)

- Keep a journal so that you can look back on how far you've come in staying focused. Journal your frustrations, growing pains, and progress.

- Protect your space. Don't let anything or anyone come into your personal space to disrupt what Jesus is doing in your life.

No one can do this for you; this is on you. You must be the one to make the decision to focus and to throw the unnecessary distractions out the door. We all are responsible for the decisions we make in life.

The focused woman
sets healthy boundaries,
will handle the unnecessary distractions in her life, and
will be intentional about hearing the still small voice.

CHAPTER 6

The Rooted Woman

Our strength lies in our roots for it is what we are rooted in that will carry us through the tumultuous seasons that we will encounter in life.

I **found myself desperately praying**, "God, please get me out of this!" But I soon realized it wasn't going to be a quick turnaround like I had anticipated. God was allowing me to go through this particular season to teach me some things, and, boy, did He teach me a lesson! He began to chip away at my preconceived ideas, and with that came an attitude adjustment. I went through the phases of frustration, kicking, screaming, and trying to force things to fit into my personal agenda, but then I finally threw my hands up and said, "Okay, God, I give up; I'm just going to hand it all over to You."

We all want things to happen in our way and in our own time, and we want it to happen now, not later. but can we trust God enough to know that, even when we are in the dark and even when we cannot see what is in front us, He still has a plan? Seasons are going to come that will mess with our faith and that will test our roots, but if we are rooted in something bigger than ourselves, we will not just survive but will overcome. It seems more often than not that as soon as we become free from one of those fiery trials, yet another trial waits to pounce, just around the corner. "Beloved, do not think it strange concerning the fiery trial which is to try you, as though some strange thing happened to you; but rejoice to the extent that you partake of Christ's sufferings, that when His glory is revealed, you may also be glad with exceeding joy" (1 Peter 4:12-13).

Perhaps one of the most challenging things in life is learning to trust God even when things don't turn out like we thought they would have or should have. Sometimes I think I have mastered this trust thing, but then another trial comes my way. I feel the burn and the pain and realize that the struggle is still very real. What keeps me sane and stops my overthinking things is the moment when I bury my head in the Word of God and meditate on a passage that pertains my season, for it sends a reminder to my soul of just how great God is. It reminds me in (Isaiah 40:8) that the grass (the tangible, what is not permanent) will wither and the flowers (persecution, disappointment, sorrow) will fall, but the Word of God lives forever. Jesus is in control. Speak this over your mind! Do not allow what's going on around you to minimize the greatness of Jesus. Do not allow the pain and suffering you experience to cause you to think that God has forgotten about you. Keep your eyes on Him! We must keep in mind that God's ways are not our ways. " 'For My thoughts are not your thoughts, nor are your ways My ways,' says the LORD" (Isaiah 55:8). This helps my perspective and gives me peace when I feel like coming unglued.

Still, I am learning.

The famous phrase "Ancora imparo," attributed to Michelangelo, means "Still, I am learning." We can all relate to this. He supposedly said this at the age of eighty-seven. I feel the same way because I am still learning as I walk through this life God has graciously given to me. I have definitely made some progress from the different experiences that I have encountered, but if I'm honest, I still have far to go. I have gone through seasons when I said, "I trust You, God," with my lips, but my actions said the opposite. At times I thought that situations would be an easy fix and that God would just basically blink an eye and set everything back to normal. Boy, was I wrong! At this juncture, I can pretty much tell you that I am no longer running through life like a deer in the headlights because every trial and test that has come my way has taught me valuable lessons. 1) I must know where I stand. 2) I must know what I am standing on.

I have felt like I was spiraling out of control and going down fast, but then I would pause for a moment and begin to say the name that is above every other name, Jesus! As soon as I called on that name, I began to feel the soft brush of His gentle hands and His peace upon my restless heart. Even though I have felt I was at the end of the rope, I have come to realize that there is always a knot at the end of the rope. I call that knot "my Lord and Savior, Jesus Christ." I call it "my Shepherd" and "my solid Rock," for He has kept me from completely falling apart. I discovered a Kurt Carr song in 2008 while in Washington, DC, "I almost let go." This song ministered to me when I was in a vulnerable and dark place and felt like letting go. Here are a few of the lyrics:

I almost let go
I felt like I couldn't take life anymore
My problems had me bound
Depression weighed me down
But God held me close
So I wouldn't let go
God's mercy kept me
So I wouldn't let go

We all need to get used to how God does things because He dances to the beat of His own drum. He (most of the time) has a different plan than our personal game plan or preference, and His timing is usually not in the timeframe that we are thinking it should be in or will be in. But we must also not give up when we find our roots being tested; instead, we must keep on going and growing. "And let us not grow weary while doing good, for in due season we shall reap if we do not lose heart" (Galatians 6:9).

Be Rooted in Something Bigger Than Yourself

You must be rooted in the Word of God if you expect to survive the heartbreaking moments, the ear-piercing seasons, and the sporadic setbacks attached to this thing called life.

As a woman who has had her roots tested in extreme forms, I have learned that I must have a strong root system because come hell or high water, I will sink if my identity is rooted in the tangible more than in the solid Rock, Christ Jesus. Make sure that your roots are rooted in something solid. Make sure that your roots are rooted in something that will not crumble under pressure.

I/we must know the Word of God.

I/we must study and meditate on the Scriptures if I/we want to survive the good, the bad, and the ugly seasons in life.

If you expect to survive and to overcome, you must be rooted in something bigger than yourself.

I feel like hitting the repeat button, staying right here just for a minute, pulling out the bullhorn, and saying it loud and clear, "You must be rooted in the Word of God if you expect to survive the heartbreaking moments, the ear-piercing seasons, and the sporadic setbacks attached to this thing called life."

Peter let us know that we can expect difficult trials and storms in life. "But may the God of all grace, who called us to His eternal glory by Christ Jesus, after you have suffered a while, perfect, establish, strengthen, and settle you" (1 Peter 5:10). The *Amplified Version* renders the last line, "will Himself complete, confirm, strengthen, and establish you [making you what you ought to be]." In this life, you will have some heartbreaking moments and will face some setbacks that take your breath, but rest assured that after you have suffered awhile, Jesus Himself will complete, confirm, strengthen, and establish you. Make sure you know where you stand, and make sure that you are standing on something solid. It's important that you are rooted in something bigger than yourself.

On Christ the solid Rock I stand.

If you expect to overcome life's hurdles, you must be rooted in Jesus Christ. The old hymn, "The Solid Rock" was penned back in 1834 by Edward Mote. I find myself singing a few lines from this hymn when I look around and see what a messy, chaotic, and confusing place the world has become. You see, it doesn't matter what kind of catastrophic events take place on earth because if we are rooted on Christ, the solid Rock, we are going to be just fine.

Here is the chorus of "The Solid Rock."

On Christ, the solid Rock, I stand;
All other ground is sinking sand,

All other ground is sinking sand.

Jesus sends a strong reminder to us in Matthew 7:24-27 of just how important it is for us to build our life on something solid. "Therefore whoever hears these sayings of Mine, and does them, I will liken him to a wise man who built his house on the rock: and the rain descended, the floods came, and the winds blew and beat on that house; and it did not fall, for it was founded on the rock. But everyone who hears these sayings of Mine, and does not do them, will be like a foolish man who built his house on the sand: and the rain descended, the floods came, and the winds blew and beat on that house; and it fell. And great was its fall."

If your roots are solid and healthy, the hellish seasons that you find yourself in will not be able to destroy you. You may slip and fall and may even find yourself flat on your face, but you will get up again. If your roots are built on the solid Rock, Christ Jesus, you will be able to weather the raging storms that come your way. Even David, whose foundation was shaken, penned this beautiful piece of poetry to encourage us to look to the Lord. "The LORD is my rock and my fortress and my deliverer; My God, my strength, in whom I will trust; My shield and the horn of my salvation, my stronghold" (Psalm 18:2).

Girlfriend, you have what it takes to be fearless, vigilant, brave, bold, focused, and rooted, but those qualities will not come without pressure.

When a trial hits your home that feels like a gigantic tsunami, devastates your relationships and emotions, and causes tremendous trauma, what you are rooted in will manifest your response and attitude. You really do find out what you are made of when you are going through a blizzard season when everything seems like a big blur and you are being tested to the point that you begin to think you are at the end. But let's park here for a moment and allow me to over-emphasize this. "Girlfriend, you have what it takes to be fearless, vigilant, brave, bold, focused, and rooted, but those qualities will not come without pressure." You see, the storms of life always test the roots of those committed to the Cross. I encourage you to stay the course even when things look grim and mucky; continue to forge ahead even when you find yourself struggling with your faith. "And He said to me, 'My grace is sufficient for you, for My strength is made perfect in weakness.' Therefore most gladly I will rather boast in my infirmities, that the power of Christ may rest upon me. Therefore I take pleasure in infirmities, in reproaches, in needs, in persecutions, in distresses for Christ's sake. For when I am weak, then I am strong" (2 Corinthians 12:9-10).

In due time, you will begin to see glimpses of the dazzling sunrays starting to sparkle through the clouds that have been wreaking havoc in your life, and you will realize that you have a lot more strength and grit than you give yourself credit for.

After enduring the many twists and turns in life, you will eventually begin to understand the significance of Matthew 28:20, "I am with you always, even to the end of the age." He will always be there to give you strength to endure the treacherous seasons. I'm reminded also that our sufferings produce endurance and that our endurance produces character. "And not only that, but we also glory in tribulations, knowing that tribulation produces perseverance; and perseverance, character; and character, hope. Now hope does not disappoint, because the love of God has been poured out in our hearts by the Holy Spirit who was given to us" (Romans 5:3-5). It's going to get a little bumpy on this journey; in fact, let's just be honest here. There will be times we are going to experience some major turbulence. In December 2019, Asbel and I were flying to California to be with my family for Christmas. It was an early flight, and our layover was in Phoenix, AZ. I was excited to see my family, and as our plane took off and headed to San Francisco, I leaned my head back and looked out the window with my music blaring in my ears. But it soon became apparent that this flight was going to shake me up a little bit. About twenty-five minutes into the flight, we found ourselves in the middle of what felt like a horrific storm. Now, keep in my mind, my husband, Asbel, had been flying two to three days a week, so he is one of those experienced fliers. I often fly myself, but this type of turbulence took what we call normal turbulence to a whole new level. We were going right and left and up and down. We dropped thousands of feet and then climbed two to four times. I have to admit that my heart rate had probably skyrocketed, along with everyone else's, and I think my hands were a little sweaty too. I saw the man in the row next to us grab the chair in front of him and clinging. I saw another lady put her head in her lap; she was shaking and probably praying. After about five minutes of this, I couldn't hold back and began to say, "Jesus!" No, it wasn't a little whisper. I heard Asbel a little bit later saying, "Jesus," too. At that point, I don't think anyone on that flight would object to my screaming, "Jesus!" This went on for probably a good twenty to twenty-five minutes, but it felt like an eternity. The flight attendants were not even able to step to the intercom to tell us to fasten our seatbelt because they could not move due the turbulence. It took everyone by surprise. But I'm pretty sure that no one on the plane needed a reminder telling them to make sure that their seatbelts were securely latched. I have to admit that I was feeling kind of scared, and I knew everyone else on the plane was feeling the same. But finally, after I had called on the name of Jesus what seemed a hundred times, the plane leveled out. Then the pilot came on with a calm voice, apologized, and said he was hopeful that we were out of the worst of it. Can I just say that when we landed in San Francisco, everyone was relieved? Asbel and I looked at each other and said, "Thank God we are on the ground."

While we were on that flight, we were in the hands of the pilot, but when the plane began to experience extreme turbulence, we began to call on the name of Jesus. Why did we call on Jesus? Because He is the only One who can get you out of your mess and who can carry you through your difficult seasons. If you are in a testing season and you're struggling with your faith, just know that suffering produces endurance, and endurance produces character. Jesus isn't going anywhere. He is on the operating table with you, He is with you in the divorce court, He is with you when the betrayal cuts deep, and He is with you when you're tired of being strong.

Make Sure Your Roots Are Healthy and Go Deep

A tree stands strong not by its fruits or branches,
but by the depth of its roots.

– Anthony Liccione

Not too long ago, my husband and I were driving back to Austin from an out-of-town trip. About an hour out, I began noticing that many of the trees looked like they had been in some kind of fire, for they were blackened. This immediately piqued my curiosity, and then I noticed that some were bent way over. It was as if they were doing all they could to stand strong, but it was obvious that they had been devastated by a traumatic event. I commented about it to Asbel, and he confirmed that, yes, a few years back a fire had broken out in that area. I noticed though that quite a few trees remained erect, and standing strong as if they were saluting their Creator. I also noticed that many of them still had green leaves on their branches, so it captured my attention. I had already been thinking about trees and their roots and so decided to do more research on this very thing. As I was reading about all the beautiful trees that that cover the earth, I was reminded that, like trees, we humans too must make sure that our roots go deep.

I found myself asking, "How do some of the trees seem to stand strong and actually survive when others around are wilting and dying?" Although I am not the most knowledgeable person on this topic, I feel I have a better understanding regarding a tree's roots. I learned that after a heavy rainfall, water saturates the ground to a deeper depth. This causes a tree's moisture-seeking roots to follow the water and therefore plant themselves deeper into the earth. It's also believed that the stress of storm winds causes the outer layers of a tree's trunk to grow faster, helping it to thicken in a shorter amount of time. George Herbert, a Welsh-born English poet and orator in the sixteenth century said it perfectly: "Storms make oaks take deeper root."

As I was studying intently on roots and trees, it became apparent that all this rooting and growing in the face of heavy weather protects a tree from simply blowing over. Of course, this doesn't mean trees are immune from damage, and yes, like humans, some die. While I lived in Louisiana, a powerful storm loomed over us, and lightning began to strike. It hit one of the big, tall trees directly behind our house. I was completely taken aback by what transpired on that stormy day. As I have studied trees, root systems, and the damage that can be done to them, I have found that not all trees hit by lightning are doomed. Actually, many do survive. The tree behind our house continued to bloom, but even though it did not look like it had a lot of external damage, it most likely was scarred. You see, we all bear scars from the lightning that tries to knock us down for good and from the storms that try to tear us apart, but like this tree, we continue to survive the hit. As we deal with the hits in life, we don't always realize how much of it goes deep inside and affects our roots. How many times have you gone through something traumatic: abuse, a co-dependent relationship, a nasty divorce, estrangement from a family member, the loss of someone you loved deeply, injustice from someone in ministry, or maybe betrayal from a good friend you had deemed as safe? You don't usually realize until later just how deep the hit went inside and how much it affected you; therefore, we must make sure that our roots run deep.

If you find yourself in a season where you are tested and feel defeated because it's been dark and gloomy for some time, I challenge you to check your root system. While going through times of great difficulty, you have to lean on what you are rooted in. The other challenge we face is keeping our attitude in check because it's easy to get testy with the Lord and the people who are around you, when you are in the throngs of a fiery trial. This has not always been an effortless thing for me to do. It takes much effort, actually, because my human side wants to reel back, fight in the flesh, and say things I should not say. But I've come to understand that when God is ready to release you from the season you are in, He will open the right door for you, and out you will go. Until then, you better hang on for dear life and lean on Jesus, and be confident enough to know that He is with you every step of the way.

Peter admonished us (1 Peter 4:12) not to be surprised at the fiery trial that tests our faith. You may be wondering, "What is a fiery trial?" A fiery trial is an ordeal that refines, purifies, and sanctifies through pressure.

"For our light affliction, which is but for a moment, is working for us a far more exceeding and eternal weight of glory" (2 Corinthians 4:17). The *Amplified Version* breaks it down a little bit more and says, "For our momentary, light distress [this passing trouble] is producing for us an eternal weight of glory [a fullness] beyond all measure [surpassing all comparisons, a transcendent splendor and an endless blessedness]!" Paul was telling the Corinthian church that he, along with his fellow servants of God, did not give up even in the face of suffering, trials, and persecution because their human weaknesses magnified the power of God as told in 2 Corinthians 4:7. They were able to endure the constant threat of death because they knew that the life of Jesus Christ would be displayed in their dying bodies (verse 11). They knew that their suffering had a purpose. The pain that Paul and all of the others had to endure helped to further the gospel and made it possible for the Corinthians to hear the gospel so that they could have eternal life. Like them, we are also facing suffering and trials. In some places around the world, great persecution takes place, but we must endure and focus on the fact that God has a purpose for our lives. Don't try to force the season to end, but allow Jesus to take you through the process. Through it you will grow into the woman of God He wants you to be.

How to have healthy roots

You might be asking, "How do I make sure that I have healthy roots and that I am doing all that I can to have a healthy root system?" Allow me to paint you a picture in a metaphor that will help you to have a better understanding of healthy roots. First, in most plants, the root system is a below-ground structure that serves primarily to anchor the plant in the soil and to take up water and minerals. Roots may be less familiar than the more visible flowers, stems, and leaves, but they are no less important to the plant.

If you want your flowers, ferns, and plants to have a healthy root system, you have to feed it nutritional things. My husband is extremely passionate about keeping our flowers, ferns, and plants watered, pruned, and tended. Now, while I may not be as passionate and knowledgeable about it, I can still water everything, and so far I do have a good track record with keeping the plants alive for a few days at least when he is out of town. We have a park-like back yard that is truly breathtaking, calming, and serene. Asbel has worked hard to keep it looking this way, and of course I help from time to time to keep the flora from dying in the Texas heat during the summer. But the one thing I have learned just by being with him outside and hearing him talk about the different plants and flowers is that sometimes they must be uprooted and replanted. They, like humans, require special nutrients in order to stay healthy.

I remember not too long ago when one of the ivy plants began turning yellow, started to droop, and looked as if it were dying. Asbel was determined to save it, so he did some research and found that it was lacking iron. As he began to feed this particular plant the proper amount of iron it needed, it began to change. It became a little bit perkier and even seemed to become more alert, and the vine is doing fine now.

We all have a choice to plant ourselves into good soil or into bad soil. So how can you have healthy roots? Remember that it takes time to develop healthy roots, so you have to start somewhere in order to get there. God doesn't want any of us to be rootless, and He has supplied the tools for us to be well-rooted along with being anchored, stable, and fruitful regardless of our climate. We all have a choice to plant ourselves into good soil or into bad soil, and in order to bear fruit we must be rooted first. No one can do it for you; you have to do it. It's your journey, and you will determine by your choices what kind of soil you are going to be rooted in.

Matthew 13 brings a parable to us about being rooted in the right soil.

Keep in mind that when Jesus told this parable, the communities all around were agriculturally based. This dynamic would have made it easier for everyone there to understand His message. Yet still this parable is made easy for all of us to grasp while at the same time convicts us to check our roots and to make sure that we are planted in the right soil.

"Then He spoke many things to them in parables, saying: 'Behold, a sower went out to sow. And as he sowed, some seed fell by the wayside; and the birds came and devoured them. Some fell on stony places, where they did not have much earth; and they immediately sprang up because they had no depth of earth. But when the sun was up they were scorched, and because they had no root they withered away. And some fell among thorns, and the thorns sprang up and choked them. But others fell on good ground and yielded a crop: some a hundredfold, some sixty, some thirty' " (Matthew 13:3-8).

In order to be rooted in good soil we must be rooted in the following:

1. **Rooted in God** - Jesus is our foundation, and we must rely solely on Him. "For no other foundation can anyone lay than that which is laid, which is Jesus Christ" (1 Corinthians 3:11). If we want to have more depth in the things of God, we must give up the shallow things that hold us back from diving deeper into godly soil. "Whoever comes to Me, and hears My sayings and does them, I will show you whom he is like: He is like a man building a house, who dug deep and laid the foundation on the rock. And when the flood arose, the stream beat vehemently

against that house, and could not shake it, for it was founded on the rock. But he who heard and did nothing is like a man who built a house on the earth without a foundation, against which the stream beat vehemently; and immediately it fell. And the ruin of that house was great" (Luke 6:47-49).

2. **Rooted in the Word of God** - The Word of God nourishes our souls that are thirsty for more. It is truly the only thing that can quench our thirst, as Psalm 42:1 says, "As the deer pants for the water brooks, So pants my soul for You, O God." In order to remain rooted in the right soil, we must be intentional about meditating on the Word of God and allowing it to go deep in our hearts so that nothing can sneak in and mess with our roots that are deeply planted in the Word of God.

But his delight is in the law of the LORD,
And in His law he meditates day and night.
He shall be like a tree
Planted by the rivers of water,
That brings forth its fruit in its season,
Whose leaf also shall not wither;
And whatever he does shall prosper
(Psalm 1:2-3).

In order to remain rooted in the Word of God, you must walk in the Spirit and not in the flesh. "I say then: Walk in the Spirit, and you shall not fulfill the lust of the flesh. For the flesh lusts against the Spirit, and the Spirit against the flesh; and these are contrary to one another, so that you do not do the things that you wish. But if you are led by the Spirit, you are not under the law" (Galatians 5:16-18). We must rightly divide the Word of God and allow it to guide us through every trial and test we experience. "Be diligent to present yourself approved to God, a worker who does not need to be ashamed, rightly dividing the word of truth" (2 Timothy 2:15).

3. **Rooted in accountability** - I read a phrase that caught my attention immediately, and I had to think about it a good minute before its meaning truly registered. "Be a river, not a swamp." Rivers have a direction and a flow. Swamps are a little different. Although streams flow in and eventually out, most of the water is directionless and stagnant, covering wide swaths of land made unusable by the marsh. You see, when people are accountable, they have a direction and a flow, but when they are not, they tend to have no direction, become stagnant, and allow voices from all directions to speak into their lives. Therefore, their roots become uprooted, contaminated, and void of the nutrients they need. When we allow ourselves to be accountable, we protect our hearts from the ravenous wolves that are ready to pounce and to devour us. When we allow ourselves to be accountable, we help ourselves to stay free from temptation and to grow our roots in good soil.

I have learned through the years that you don't need a ton of confidantes and accountability partners. Not everyone needs to know about the junk and stuff in your closet, but if you have just one or two people to whom you are accountable, then you are in a good place. "Therefore, confess your sins to one another [your false steps, your offenses], and pray for one another, that you may be healed and restored. The heartfelt and persistent prayer of a righteous man (believer) can accomplish much [when put into action and made effective by God—it is dynamic and can have tremendous power]" (James 5:16).

We should already be telling God about all of the junk, temptations, mistakes, and sins in our lives, but this verse tells us to confess these things to one another. In return, our confidantes and accountability partners will hold us accountable so that we will not repeat the same mistakes and give in to the temptations that surround us every day. This will help us to stay rooted in good soil.

Deep roots will keep us steady through the trials of life.

We women need to have a healthy root system that will carry us through every hardship that comes our way. Our roots are very important to us because they will shape how we think, act, and grow. Without the proper root system, we tend to vacillate and waver under pressure. Through the process, our roots (good or bad) speak to us, so this is the perfect time to rid ourselves of the things that hinder us from being completely rooted in Jesus Christ. God's Word tells us to purify ourselves from everything that contaminates the body and spirit, perfecting holiness out of reverence for God (2 Corinthians 7:1). *The Message* emphasizes it little more and tells us to make a clean break from everything that defiles and distracts us. It's time to make a change and to break free from the things that threaten to destroy our healthy roots. Do you know what you are rooted in?

Is your identity wrapped up in your successes, your platform, your brand, another person, or an organization, or is it completely rooted in Jesus Christ?

We must learn to stand on our own two feet and have a life-changing Jesus moment so that, when we do have to stand alone for our faith, we are going to stand even if it means persecution, ridicule, or loss of our prestigious positions and fame.

The world is in a huge mess, but if we are rooted in the solid Rock, Christ Jesus, we will continue to be victorious. As we look around, we see events occurring that most of us probably thought we would never see in our lifetime, and it's happening right before our eyes. Morals seem to be crumbling all around us, and division, tension, and hateful rhetoric spew out of the mouths of many. It seems the earth is shaking. You see rampant racism and corruption everywhere you look; it's as if the world has lost its mind. Our roots are being tested like never before, and I have a feeling that this is just the beginning of things to come. But we must recognize that, no matter what comes our way, this world is not our home. Oh, I know that that sounds a bit faddish and like a good ol' catch phrase, but nevertheless it is true. Indeed, this world is not our permanent home. If we keep this in mind, our perspective will remain focused on God's will instead of ours to be done on earth as it is in heaven (Matthew 6:10).

Think about it: God has allowed you and me to be right here this very moment! He called us to fulfill His plan and to execute His vision during these unprecedented times. We are here for a purpose, we are here for something that is bigger than ourselves, and we must make sure that we are rooted in something bigger than ourselves so that we will be able to withstand whatever comes against us. Since this world is not our permanent home and we are here on a God assignment, we must shine brightly in this dark world and reach the broken, the vulnerable, the oppressed, the wounded, and the confused souls for Him. Matthew 5:14 tells us that we are the light of the world, and verse 16 adds, "Let your light so shine before men, that they may see your good works and glorify your Father in heaven."

You can do this! "For we are God's handiwork, created in Christ Jesus to do good works, which God prepared in advance for us to do" (Ephesians 2:10, NIV).

You were built for this! "Blessed is the man who endures temptation; for when he has been approved, he will receive the crown of life which the Lord has promised to those who love Him" (James 1:12).

Your Roots Are Going to Be Tested

The early church's roots went deep, and no matter the amount of pressure, persecution, and painful experiences they had to endure, they continued to thrive.

Paul's roots were tested, but we see quickly that his allegiance to Jesus Christ was more important than anything else. In fact, as we read the entire New Testament, it's very clear that the disciples in that era were completely sold out for the cause of Jesus Christ and were completely committed to fulfilling the vision that God had for them, regardless of the pain and suffering that they had to endure. Their allegiance was not to the Roman Empire, a group of people, or any type of leader, but they were solely committed to Jesus Christ. In fact, they had such a holy reverence for Christ that they were extremely careful to not build their own empires or platforms that would bring glory to them. Everything they did on earth always pointed to Jesus Christ. "As Peter was coming in, Cornelius met him and fell down at his feet and worshiped him. But Peter lifted him up, saying, 'Stand up; I myself am also a man' " (Acts 10:25-26). Peter was not about to start a trend in allowing someone to worship him instead of Jesus Christ. He nipped that quickly and then moved on because he was rooted in something bigger than himself. Peter also said (2 Peter 3:18), "But grow in the grace and knowledge of our Lord and Savior Jesus Christ. To him be the glory both now and forever. Amen." In the current climate, we need to make sure that our allegiance is to Jesus Christ alone because there is no one else who can save us, restore us, and deliver us. Only Jesus can do these things. Paul said in 2 Timothy 4:7-8: "I have fought the good fight, I have finished the race, I have kept the faith. Finally, there is laid up for me the crown of righteousness, which the Lord, the righteous Judge, will give to me on that Day, and not to me only but also to all who have loved His appearing." Paul was completely focused on reaching people from all walks of life, and at the end of his life he was able to say, "I have fought the good fight, and I have kept the faith."

There is power in the name of Jesus

What I find so incredibly fascinating about Saul, who later became the apostle Paul, is how sold out he was to the cause of destroying the Christians. He was hell-bent on destroying the message of Jesus Christ. But his abrupt turnaround from being a zealous persecutor of Christians to one of Christianity's greatest proponents lets us know just how powerful the name of Jesus is. We read about his conversion that changed the trajectory of his entire life (Acts 9). Saul was confronted by the very One whom he was persecuting. He was passionate about persecuting God's people, but a great transformation that took place in his life. "As he neared Damascus on his journey, suddenly a light from heaven flashed around him. He fell to the ground and heard a voice say to him, 'Saul, Saul, why do you persecute me?' 'Who are you, Lord?' Saul asked. 'I am Jesus, whom you are persecuting,' he replied" (Acts 9:3-5, NIV). After that intense and life-changing moment, he went from Saul to Paul and never turned back to his old ways. He was never the same after that incredible encounter with Jesus Christ.

Paul was completely sold out to the cause of Jesus Christ, but with that ministry came lots of trials, persecution, and suffering. As we view his life from the Scriptures, it's evident that he too was rooted in something bigger than himself. He was rooted in a name that was sovereign and the Cross, and no matter how much suffering he had to endure, he continued to fight the good fight of faith. Keep in mind that 2 Timothy 4:7-8 doesn't say Paul fought the perfect fight of faith, so don't discredit yourself when you do struggle in the good fight of faith. None of us are perfect, for we will fall down and mess up. But then we must allow ourselves to fall into the arms of Jesus, for only He is perfect and only He can help us with our imperfections. When you fall and slip up, get back into the saddle again, and gallop your way into a healthier lifestyle that will keep you rooted. When it seems as if all hell is coming against you, you will be able to stand strong against the enemy's ploys. Paul was tested, but his roots went deep. They were built on Christ, the solid Rock!

It's not always going to be a rosy garden.

You may feel hard-pressed and even perplexed at times, but that isn't a recipe for failure. Paul's life was not a rosy garden; it was far from being glamorous. It was gruesome and difficult at times, and he was challenged and hunted by men who wanted to destroy him for what he believed and preached. Acts 23 relates that more than forty men conspired to not eat or drink until they murdered Paul. Can you imagine being Paul and knowing that they wanted to destroy you for preaching about the name of Jesus? But Paul along with the other disciples remained devoted to Jesus. Even if it meant death, they were not fazed or intimidated by the threats but continued to preach the gospel of Jesus Christ. Many supernatural things took place in Paul's life and in the lives of the other disciples, for they were completely sold out to Christ no matter the cost. They knew the power of Jesus in their lives, and He continued to use them, to anoint them, and to operate through them with miracles, signs, and wonders. Their faith was in a higher power, Jesus Christ!

Those of us who live in Western civilization sometimes find it difficult to fathom the masses who have been persecuted for the cause of Jesus Christ and who are persecuted and even killed for it today. We have (so far) been able to live pretty comfortably as Christians. We have not been silenced in speaking the name of Jesus. We can wear crosses around our necks, carry our Bibles, buy Scripture quotes on pretty planks, and even purchase cute coffee mugs that have verses printed on them. We can go to the local coffee shops, open our Bibles, and have a Bible study with friends. We can talk to people in the grocery store about God's goodness, and we can even put bumper stickers on our cars with Bible verses and the name, Jesus. Thus, when we hear Paul talk about suffering, we get the feeling that he spoke as a man who suffered even more than he described in his letters.

We are hard-pressed on every side, yet not crushed; we are perplexed, but not in despair; persecuted, but not forsaken; struck down, but not destroyed—always carrying about in the body the dying of the Lord Jesus, that the life of Jesus also may be manifested in our body. For we who live are always delivered to death for Jesus' sake, that the life of Jesus also may be manifested in our mortal flesh. So then death is working in us, but life in you (2 Corinthians 4:8-12).

We are hard pressed (troubled) – Paul used this word first. He made sure to put "we" in the first verse so that we can get a better understanding of the Christians' ordeals during that time. He referred to some of the trials that he and his fellow laborers, along with the original disciples, experienced to make the gospel known to the world. The disciples were tested with their faith constantly, but it's obvious that their roots were embedded deep at the foot of the Cross. Nothing could remove their eyes from the great commission (Matthew 28:16-20) that had been set before them. Nothing the Roman Empire—or for that matter, a governor, king, or member of the religious elite—could say or do influenced them to give up their Jesus assignments. They were in it for the long haul, and their roots would always trump every pressure, every hurt, and every misunderstanding, as well as every type of persecution they would have to endure. Their faith was unshakable! Nothing could derail them, and regardless of the hellish seasons that they went through, they stayed the course.

Get rid of the weeds in your life.

I'd like to think that I have deep, healthy roots, but this past year has challenged me on a whole new level. Seriously, there have been times when I have not been sure if I've been running with a football, basketball, or soccer ball or just throwing a dodge ball over the cliff. That is how crazy this year has been. Through this, I've had to dig deep into my root system and even had to cut some things off at the root that were trying to sneak in to blend in with my healthy roots. You better be quick on your feet because there are lots of sneaky, sly, and deceptive weeds that are fixated on contaminating your healthy roots. As Christian women, we need to self-reflect and do some inventory in our lives; we need to do some soul-searching to make sure that we have not been glossing over the weeds in our lives. How many toxic weeds have taken root in our own lives, and we didn't even realize it until we started experiencing the repercussions? Guess what? They will continue to come, so you must be ready to nip them at the root. In order to have healthy roots so that we can be productive, we will need to be on the lookout for any weeds that make their way into our personal space. This is similar to how we deal with weeds in a garden. Weeds will steal light and nutrients from the plants we want to grow, and they will also crowd out space needed for the crops to flourish. All it takes is one small weed to corrupt, so you need to be on alert at all times.

Song of Solomon 2:15 reminds us to take care of the little foxes that come in and try to spoil the vine. Of course, a little fox seems harmless, right? Typically, foxes are small animals, about twenty inches long, and the average Middle Eastern fox weighs only about eight or nine pounds. Foxes are quick and skillful but are not strong like a coyote, nor are they dangerous like a bear. You can't even compare a fox to a huge animal like an elephant in Africa, which can trample whole fields in just a few hours. Foxes are fairly small animals, yet the little fox is capable of doing terrible damage. They burrow and chew in a vineyard until the vines wither and become unproductive. Similar to weeds, they (metaphorically) can destroy your life if you do not handle them in a timely manner. Weeds and foxes have one thing in common: they are resilient and stubborn and don't give up easily. The enemy of our soul also doesn't give up easily, so you must be intentional about recognizing the unhealthy things that try to become a part of your life. Nip those intruders in the bud.

Trees have to have strong roots to survive, and so do we. As a matter of fact, in order for trees to be fruitful, their roots must go deep into the ground. But they require more than just deep roots; they must have healthy roots. When your roots are healthy, you will be able to discern when a weed (the wrong voices, influences, offenses, negativity, pride, arrogance, self-righteousness, jealousy, or lust) has sneaked into your personal space and is trying to contaminate your root system. Be purposeful with building a strong root system even if it means that you have to say good-bye to some unhealthy things that have been sucking the life out of you. The reason why many Christians struggle to have healthy roots is because we have failed to discern the difference between healthy roots and destructive roots. The symptoms of an illness tend to show up long before the root cause is revealed. The same goes for our spiritual health. We are given signs that something is off, but oftentimes we ignore them. "The heart is deceitful above all things And it is extremely sick; Who can understand it fully and know its secret motives?" (Jeremiah 17:9). While the immediate context here is the nation of Judah, that nation also illustrates the human condition of everyone everywhere. The only way to make sure that our roots go deep and remain healthy is to become completely reliant on our Lord and Savior, Jesus Christ, and on His Word. In addition, we must remain vigilant about keeping our hearts pure from the toxicity in the world.

The weeds of life have made their way in and have become good at wearing a façade. The less we pray, the more we lack discernment; the less we apply Scripture to our situation, the more we fail to see that our roots are being bludgeoned by the world's system. The less we seek God's face, the more we are deceived by the very same serpent that charmed his way into Eve's life. My father used to have a saying that I feel bears repeating, "The church cannot do business as usual." In other words, we cannot do life as usual. There is a real devil who is trying to wreak havoc in our lives and who is trying to destroy our healthy roots. He would love to see you fall apart and never do anything productive for God. He would love to destroy your confidence in loving someone else again because of the betrayal and rejection you dealt with in a previous marriage or relationship. He would love for you to throw in the towel on your calling and call it quits. Don't do it! Instead, fight the urge to give up. Take care of the weeds in your life so that you can have healthy roots that will flourish for the kingdom of God.

Roots are essential for the plant, flower, and tree to have life; therefore, having a connection with Christ is absolutely a necessity if we want to live life abundantly. If we want to live a life that is pleasing to Christ, we must be rooted in Him.

What are some of the benefits of being rooted in Christ?

1. Stability. When you are rooted in Christ, you will not be shaken by the storms of life, nor will you be tempted to succumb to every shifting of doctrine that comes your way." The enemy creates instability, so having deep roots will sustain you through the seasons of drought and difficulties and will also help you to remain faithful and focused on your God assignments. "But the Lord is faithful, who will establish you and guard you from the evil one" (2 Thessalonians 3:3). "Let us hold fast the confession of our faith without wavering, for He who promised is faithful" (Hebrews 10:23).

2. Spiritual growth. You will grow spiritually and become a mature Christian. "When I was a child, I spoke as a child, I understood as a child, I thought as a child; but when I became a [woman], I put away childish things" (1 Corinthians 13:11). Children are easily influenced by anything and everything, but when they reach maturity, they are finally able to differentiate between right and wrong. When we are spiritually mature, we will no longer be easily influenced, and we will also be able to discern the erroneous voices in our midst that are not in sync with the Word of God. "So that we are no longer

children [spiritually immature], tossed back and forth [like ships on a stormy sea] and carried about by every wind of [shifting] doctrine, by the cunning and trickery of [unscrupulous] men, by the deceitful scheming of people ready to do anything [for personal profit]. But speaking the truth in love [in all things—both our speech and our lives expressing His truth], let us grow up in all things into Him [following His example] who is the Head—Christ" (Ephesians 4:14-15).

3. Influence. Being rooted will help you to become influential for the kingdom of God. If you want to influence others for Him, your words and your actions will show them. Being rooted in Christ will help us with our behaviors, our attitudes, and our words so that we can exemplify Jesus Christ and influence others to turn their hearts toward Him. "Keep your behavior excellent among the [unsaved] Gentiles [conduct yourself honorably, with graciousness and integrity], so that for whatever reason they may slander you as evildoers, yet by observing your good deeds they may [instead come to] glorify God in the day of visitation [when He looks upon them with mercy]" (1 Peter 2:12). "As you have therefore received Christ Jesus the Lord, so walk in him, rooted and built up in Him and established in the faith, as you have been taught, abounding in it with thanksgiving" (Colossians 2:6-7). When we are rooted in Christ, our speech, behaviors, and attitudes will reveal our source of life.

I wrote the following poem during the pandemic.

She stands tall, determined to not cower to the wind.
The wind begins to blow feverishly, and she feels herself losing
balance.
But she digs her heels into the solid ground beneath her even more.
She tells herself, "I'm not going down without a fight!"
She hears the loud banging and clanging as she is watching
the debris flying around in the wind.
It's almost as if the wind is taunting her with a haunting type
song and telling her
that she will never make it to the other side.
But again she braces herself against the forces of nature
and pushes on through.
She tells herself again, "I'm not going down without a fight!"
"I don't care what the statistics say."
"I don't care what the diagnosis is telling me."
"I don't care if I have to do this alone; I refuse to give up."
But the storm continues to rage on, and the wind mixed with the
downpour of
rain begins to flood her troubled mind.
She feels herself weakening and is weary from the elements of the
storm.
She thinks that maybe it is over, and maybe she should lay down
and die.
But then she hears the whisper, "Try one more time."
She replies in a voice that is barely above a whisper, "But, God, I
am tired of the fight."
He responds to her with the gentlest voice that's ever been
known, "My daughter, I will give you strength for the journey,
and I will never leave you nor forsake you."

The cares of life rain on us until we sometimes feel we are drowning. The battle rages on whether we think we are ready or not. The diagnosis sometimes gets inside our head and causes fear to permeate our thoughts. The hurt, which we thought we were over, rears its ugly head again and brings up old memories. The past tries to tell us that we aren't qualified to be fearless women of God. . . . But it's high time that we take a stand; become vigilant, prayerful, brave, bold, focused, and rooted; and commit 100 percent to being fearless women for the kingdom of God!

The rooted woman
knows where she stands and
knows what she stands on;
she is rooted on Christ, the solid Rock.

Made in the USA
Monee, IL
19 May 2026

50456349R00115